GoodFood
Simple suppers

First published 2003
Published by BBC Books,
an imprint of Ebury Publishing
A Random House Group Company

Photographs © BBC Magazines 2003
Recipes © BBC Magazines 2003
Book design © Woodlands Books Ltd 2003
All recipes contained within this book first appeared in BBC *Good Food*
magazine and BBC *Vegetarian Good Food* magazine.

The Random House Group Limited Reg. No. 954009

Addresses for companies within the Random House Group can be found
at www.randomhouse.co.uk

A CIP catalogue record for this book is available from the British Library

The Random House Group Limited supports The Forest Stewardship
Council (FSC), the leading international forest certification organization. All
our titles that are printed on Greenpeace approved FSC certified paper
carry the FSC logo. Our paper procurement policy can be found at
www.rbooks.co.uk/environment

To buy books by your favourite authors and register for offers visit
www.rbooks.co.uk

Edited by Gilly Cubitt
Commissioning Editor: Vivien Bowler
Project Editor: Sarah Miles
Designers: Kathryn Gammon and Annette Peppis
Design Manager: Sarah Ponder
Jacket Design: Kathryn Gammon
Production: Christopher Tinker

Printed and bound by Firmengruppe APPL, aprinta druck,
Wemding, Germany

ISBN: 9780563488422

40 39 38 37 36 35 34 33 32 31

easy GoodFood
Simple suppers

Editor Orlando Murrin

BOOKS

Contents

`

Introduction   6

Introduction

Our busy lifestyles mean we have less and less time for cooking. Yet our tastes are becoming more sophisticated. That's why at *BBC Good Food Magazine* we have compiled this delectable collection of simple suppers, bringing you a selection of exciting dishes to liven up your repertoire.

Whether you want Middle Eastern spices or the fresh flavours of the Mediterranean, all our recipes use ingredients that you'll have in your storecupboard or find at your local supermarket. They're easy to cook, even for beginners, and won't cost the earth.

Our cookery teams have made sure preparation is kept to a minimum; in fact many of these dishes are pop-in-the-oven one pots or quick stir fries. And each recipe comes with a nutritional breakdown so you can look out for the calorie, fat and salt content.

Before you think you don't have time for cooking, we've ensured most of the dishes, including the *Pizza Jackets* pictured opposite (see page 52 for recipe), can be cooked in under 30 minutes. These recipes are serious competition for ready meals – and you'll certainly taste the difference.

Orlando Murrin

Editor, *BBC Good Food Magazine*

Conversion tables

NOTES ON THE RECIPES
• Eggs are medium in the UK and Australia (large in America) unless stated otherwise.
• Wash all fresh produce before preparation.

OVEN TEMPERATURES

Gas	°C	Fan °C	°F	Oven temp.
¼	110	90	225	Very cool
½	120	100	250	Very cool
1	140	120	275	Cool or slow
2	150	130	300	Cool or slow
3	160	140	325	Warm
4	180	160	350	Moderate
5	190	170	375	Moderately hot
6	200	180	400	Fairly hot
7	220	200	425	Hot
8	230	210	450	Very hot
9	240	220	475	Very hot

APPROXIMATE WEIGHT CONVERSIONS
• All the recipes in this book list both imperial and metric measurements. Conversions are approximate and have been rounded up or down. Follow one set of measurements only; do not mix the two.
• Cup measurements, which are used by cooks in Australia and America, have not been listed here as they vary from ingredient to ingredient. Please use kitchen scales to measure dry/solid ingredients.

SPOON MEASURES

• Spoon measurements are level unless otherwise specified.

• 1 teaspoon = 5ml

• 1 tablespoon = 15ml

• 1 Australian tablespoon = 20ml (cooks in Australia should measure 3 teaspoons where 1 tablespoon is specified in a recipe)

APPROXIMATE LIQUID CONVERSIONS

metric	imperial	AUS	US
50ml	2fl oz	¼ cup	¼ cup
125ml	4fl oz	½ cup	½ cup
175ml	6fl oz	¾ cup	¾ cup
225ml	8fl oz	1 cup	1 cup
300ml	10fl oz/½ pint	½ pint	1¼ cups
450ml	16fl oz	2 cups	2 cups/1 pint
600ml	20fl oz/1 pint	1 pint	2½ cups
1 litre	35fl oz/1¾ pints	1¾ pints	1 quart

To make the croûtons, toss bread cubes in oil and bake in a hot oven for 10–12 minutes until crisp, topping with cheese halfway through.

Vegetable and Cheese Soup

25g/1oz butter
1 tbsp olive oil
1 onion, chopped
1 potato, about 225g/8oz, chopped
2 sticks celery, chopped
550g/1lb 4oz mixed root vegetables, such as potato, swedes, parsnips and carrots, chopped
1 litre/1¾ pints vegetable stock
140g/5oz mature cheddar
1 tbsp wholegrain mustard
cheesy croûtons, to serve

Takes 50 minutes • Serves 4

1 Heat the butter and oil in a large pan. Add the onion and cook until golden. Add the other vegetables and stir. Season, cover, reduce the heat and cook for 10 minutes, stirring occasionally, until just tender.
2 Pour the stock into the pan, bring to the boil, then cover and simmer for 20 minutes until the vegetables are softened. Whizz in a food processor until smooth. Meanwhile, grate half the cheese and cut the rest into small cubes.
3 Reheat the soup in the pan and stir in most of the grated cheese and all the cubes, until the cheese begins to melt. Stir in the mustard and season. Sprinkle with cheesy croûtons and the remaining cheese.

• Per serving 320 kcalories, protein 13g, carbohydrate 21g, fat 21g, saturated fat 11g, fibre 4g, added sugar none, salt 1.78g

Use a jar of satay (peanut) sauce
as a base to make this simple soup.

Vegetable Satay Soup

450g/1lb new potatoes
1 carrot
175g/6oz green beans
1 vegetable stock cube
100g/4oz podded broad beans
(or frozen or canned)
330ml jar satay sauce
175g/6oz cherry tomatoes, halved
pitta bread, to serve

Takes 20 minutes • Serves 4

1 Cut the potatoes into 2.5cm/1in chunks
(no need to peel). Quarter the carrot
lengthways, then cut across into small
pieces. Trim the green beans, then cut into
short sticks.
2 Put the potatoes and carrot in a medium
pan with 850ml/1½ pints water and the
stock cube. Bring to the boil, stir to dissolve
the cube, then simmer, covered, for
10–12 minutes until the vegetables are
almost tender. Tip in the green and broad
beans and simmer for 2 minutes.
3 Pour in the satay sauce and simmer for
3–4 minutes. Stir in the tomatoes. Serve with
warm pitta bread.

• Per serving 596 kcalories, protein 19g, carbohydrate
40g, fat 42g, saturated fat 9g, fibre 10g, added sugar
6g, salt 3.27g

This is a really light, subtle soup with fresh vibrant flavours. Serve it without the rice as a starter.

Hot-sour Coconut Soup

100g/4oz Thai fragrant rice
1.2 litres/2 pints chicken or vegetable stock
1 stalk of lemongrass, thinly sliced
1 tbsp finely chopped galangal or fresh root ginger
4 fresh or freeze-dried kaffir lime leaves, chopped or crumbled
2 red chillies, seeded and finely chopped
250g/9oz boneless skinless chicken breast, thinly sliced
175g/6oz chestnut mushrooms, sliced
225g/8oz cherry tomatoes, halved
1 tbsp lime juice
2 tbsp fish sauce (*nam pla*)
200ml carton coconut cream
a handful of fresh coriander, chopped

Takes 30 minutes • Serves 4

1 Cook the rice in salted boiling water for about 10 minutes, until tender, then drain and set aside.

2 Meanwhile, heat the stock in a large pan, add the lemongrass, galangal or ginger, lime leaves and chillies and simmer for 5 minutes. Add the chicken and mushrooms and simmer for a further 5 minutes.

3 Stir in the tomatoes, lime juice, fish sauce and coconut cream and simmer for 5 minutes more. Scatter over the coriander and serve each portion with a little cooked rice spooned in.

• Per serving 356 kcalories, protein 22g, carbohydrate 26g, fat 19g, saturated fat 15g, fibre 1g, added sugar none, salt 2.47g

It's worth buying mozzarella made from
buffalo milk, not cow's milk, for this salad.

Tricolore Salad with Lemon Dressing

225g/8oz buffalo mozzarella
2 large firm ripe tomatoes
40g bag rocket

FOR THE DRESSING
½ lemon
good pinch of sea salt
½ tsp freshly ground black pepper
4 tbsp extra virgin olive oil

Takes 20 minutes • Serves 4

1 Cut the mozzarella and tomatoes into slices of an equal thickness. Arrange alternate slices of mozzarella and tomato on four side plates. Put a pile of rocket leaves beside each.

2 Pare the lemon using a lemon zester to make small thin strips of peel. (If you don't have a zester, use a sharp knife to pare off strips of the rind, taking care not to include any white pith, then cut the strips into minute strands.) Squeeze the juice from the lemon into a bowl and add the sea salt and black pepper. Whisk, gradually mixing in the olive oil until the dressing is thickened.

3 Drizzle the lemon dressing over the rocket, mozzarella and tomato on the plates, then scatter over the lemon strips and serve.

• Per serving 260 kcalories, protein 14g, carbohydrate 3g, fat 22g, saturated fat 8g, fibre 1g, added sugar none, salt 1.04g

There's no need to cook the couscous –
just soak it and mix in the tasty bits.

Mediterranean Couscous Salad

225g/8oz couscous
400ml/14fl oz vegetable stock
10 sun-dried or sunblush
tomatoes, quartered
2 medium avocados, peeled, stoned
and cut into large chunks
100g/4oz black olives
a good handful of nuts, such as pine
nuts, cashews or almonds
225g/8oz feta, roughly crumbled
130g bag green salad leaves

FOR THE DRESSING
5 tbsp olive oil
2 tbsp lemon juice

Takes 20 minutes • Serves 4
(easily halved)

1 Tip the couscous into a large bowl, stir in the stock, cover and leave to soak for 5 minutes.
2 Make the dressing by whisking together the olive oil, lemon juice and seasoning. Stir two tablespoons into the couscous, then gently mix in the tomatoes, avocados, olives, nuts and feta. Taste for seasoning.
3 Toss the salad leaves with the remaining dressing, divide between four plates and spoon the couscous on top.

• Per serving 636 kcalories, protein 14g, carbohydrate 29g, fat 52g, saturated fat 11g, fibre 4g, added sugar none, salt 3.82g

Crisp and tangy, chicory adds a soft tang to salads.
Just pull off the leaves and discard the core.

Cheddar and Chicory Salad

FOR THE DRESSING
5 tbsp olive oil
2 tsp clear honey
1 tbsp wholegrain mustard
2 tbsp lemon juice

FOR THE SALAD
225g/8oz chicory
1 red-skinned apple
85g/3oz walnut pieces
100g/4oz mature cheddar

Takes 20 minutes • Serves 4

1 To make the dressing, put all the ingredients into a small bowl and blend thoroughly with a small whisk or fork. Season to taste and set aside.
2 Separate the chicory leaves and divide between four plates. Cut the apple into quarters, core and thinly slice. Scatter the apple slices over the chicory and sprinkle with the walnuts.
3 Using a vegetable peeler, make cheddar shavings and scatter over each serving. Drizzle the dressing over the salad and finish with a grating of black pepper.

• Per serving 441 kcalories, protein 10g, carbohydrate 9g, fat 38g, saturated fat 9g, fibre 2g, added sugar 2g, salt 0.59g

A simple salad but one with plenty of contrasting textures.
You'll find Caesar dressing in most supermarkets.

Warm Caesar-style Salad

6 medium eggs
140g/5oz green beans, trimmed
1 ciabatta loaf
2 tbsp extra virgin olive oil
50g/2oz parmesan, finely grated,
plus extra shavings to garnish
1 cos lettuce, roughly chopped
ready-made Caesar dressing

Takes 30 minutes • Serves 4

1 Preheat the grill. Bring a pan of water to the boil, carefully drop in the eggs and cook for 4 minutes. Place in cold water to cool. Cook the green beans in lightly salted boiling water for 4 minutes until tender. Drain well and place in a large salad bowl.
2 Cut the ciabatta loaf into large cubes and toss in the oil and the parmesan. Tip the bread on to a baking tray and grill, turning, until golden.
3 Peel the eggs and cut into four lengthways. Add the croûtons and lettuce to the beans. Season and mix well. Pile on to serving plates and top with the eggs. Drizzle over the dressing and top with the parmesan shavings.

• Per serving 684 kcalories, protein 27g, carbohydrate 67g, fat 36g, saturated fat 8g, fibre 4g, added sugar none, salt 2.68g

This colourful salad travels well in a lunchbox.
Try other beans and cheeses in combination too.

Cannellini Bean Salad

1 small red onion
1 red or yellow pepper
400g can cannellini beans
4 tbsp ready-made vinaigrette
½ iceberg or 1 cos lettuce
250g packet feta
warm Italian bread, to serve

Takes 10 minutes • Serves 4

1 Halve and finely slice the onion and pepper. Drain and rinse the beans. Put the ingredients in a salad bowl.

2 Add the vinaigrette and mix well. Tear the lettuce leaves straight into the bowl.

3 Break the feta into chunks, throw into the salad and season with black pepper. Serve with warm Italian bread.

• Per serving 348 kcalories, protein 16g, carbohydrate 17g, fat 25g, saturated fat 10g, fibre 4g, added sugar none, salt 2.57g

A jar of marinated feta cubes from the supermarket cheese counter provides the protein and the dressing.

Chickpea and Feta Salad

1 cucumber, thickly sliced
1 small red onion, thinly sliced
300g jar marinated feta cubes in oil
4 large tomatoes, cut into wedges
420g can chickpeas, drained and rinsed
few black olives
juice of ½ lemon
2 little gem lettuces

TO SERVE
4 pitta breads
1 spring onion, chopped

Takes 15 minutes, plus draining • Serves 4

1 Put the cucumber and onion in a sieve over a bowl, sprinkle with salt and leave to drain for 20 minutes. Drain the cheese cubes, reserving the oil.
2 Preheat the grill. Toss the cucumber and onion with the tomatoes, chickpeas, olives, cheese, three tablespoons of the oil and the lemon juice. Season. Line salad bowls with the lettuce leaves and pile the salad on top.
3 Grill the pitta on one side, turn over and brush with a little oil from the cheese. Sprinkle the spring onion over and grill until crisp. Serve with the salad.

• Per serving 637 kcalories, protein 28g, carbohydrate 67g, fat 31g, saturated fat 11g, fibre 8g, added sugar none, salt 4.37g

With the main ingredients bought ready-cooked,
you've only got the potatoes to do.

Warm Mackerel and Beetroot Salad

450g/1lb new potatoes, cut into
bite-size pieces
3 smoked mackerel fillets, skinned
250g pack cooked beetroot
120g bag mixed salad leaves
2 celery sticks, finely sliced
50g/2oz walnut pieces

FOR THE DRESSING
3 tbsp walnut oil
2 tbsp sunflower oil
2 tbsp fresh lemon juice
2 tsp creamed horseradish sauce

Takes 20 minutes • Serves 4
(easily halved)

1 Cook the potatoes in salted boiling water for 12–15 minutes until just tender. Meanwhile, flake the mackerel fillets into large pieces. Cut the beetroot into bite-sized chunks.

2 Drain the potatoes and cool slightly. Mix together all the dressing ingredients and season. Tip in the potatoes.

3 Add the salad leaves, mackerel, beetroot, celery and walnuts. Pour over the dressing and toss well. Serve warm.

• Per serving 634 kcalories, protein 22g, carbohydrate 26g, fat 50g, saturated fat 2g, fibre 4g, added sugar none, salt 1.91g

This recipe is easily multiplied to feed
a crowd as part of a buffet.

Oriental Prawn and Pasta Salad

100g/4oz fresh beansprouts
250g/9oz fresh tagliatelle
2 carrots, cut into thin sticks
1 bunch spring onions,
cut into shreds
¼ cucumber, cut into thin ribbons
with a potato peeler
225g/8oz cooked peeled prawns
5 tbsp sunflower oil
2 tbsp light soy sauce
2 tbsp rice vinegar or
white wine vinegar
1 tbsp finely chopped fresh
root ginger
1 large garlic clove, crushed
1 tsp clear honey
sesame oil, to serve

Takes 30 minutes • Serves 4

1 Put the beansprouts in a bowl, cover with cold water and leave for 10 minutes, then drain (this crisps them up). Meanwhile cook the pasta in a pan of salted boiling water according to the packet instructions.
2 Tip the pasta into a colander and run under the cold tap, then drain thoroughly. Toss with the carrots, spring onions, cucumber, prawns and beansprouts.
3 For the dressing, whisk together the sunflower oil, soy sauce, vinegar, ginger, garlic and honey. Pour over the pasta and lightly toss. Drizzle with a little sesame oil to serve.

• Per serving 439 kcalories, protein 21g, carbohydrate 54g, fat 17g, saturated fat 2g, fibre 4g, added sugar 1g, salt 3.42g

The runner-bean season is a precious time so make the most of it. Buy the beans on the day you intend to eat them, if possible.

Runner Bean and Bacon Salad

450g/1lb runner beans, cut into fine slivers
100g/4oz good quality streaky bacon, cut into strips
2 tbsp sherry vinegar or white wine vinegar
4 tbsp extra virgin olive oil
1 tbsp wholegrain mustard
140g/5oz cherry tomatoes, halved, or small tomatoes, cut into wedges

Takes 20 minutes • Serves 4

1 Blanch the runner beans in a large pan of salted boiling water for 3 minutes, then drain and cool under cold running water. Drain well and transfer to a serving bowl.

2 Heat a frying pan, then add the bacon and let it sizzle until crisp. Remove from the pan and set aside. Stir the vinegar and oil into the hot pan and warm through, then whisk in the mustard. Pour the warm dressing over the beans.

3 Toss in the tomatoes, then season well. Garnish with the crispy bacon and serve warm.

• Per serving 204 kcalories, protein 6g, carbohydrate 5g, fat 18g, saturated fat 4g, fibre 3g, added sugar none, salt 1.22g

Choose a soft, ripe camembert and
let it rest at room temperature before using.

Bacon and Camembert Salad

8 rashers smoked streaky bacon
125g pack camembert
2 thick slices bread (about 85g/3oz),
crusts removed
7 tbsp olive oil
140g bag crisp green salad
2 tbsp white wine vinegar
1 tbsp wholegrain mustard
1 garlic clove, finely chopped

Takes 15 minutes • Serves 4

1 Preheat the grill and cook the bacon for 5–8 minutes until crisp, turning halfway through. Set aside to cool. Cut the camembert into bite-size wedges.

2 Grate the bread into coarse crumbs. Heat two tablespoons of the oil in a frying pan and cook the crumbs, stirring, until crisp and golden. Season and set aside.

3 Tip the salad into a bowl. Break the bacon into bite-size pieces and mix into the salad with the cheese. Mix together the vinegar, mustard, garlic and remaining olive oil. Pour over the salad and toss well. Sprinkle with the crisp crumbs and serve.

• Per serving 465 kcalories, protein 17g, carbohydrate 12g, fat 39g, saturated fat 12g, fibre 1g, added sugar none, salt 2.56g

Buy a thick slice of ham from the
deli counter for a chunky finish.

Peach, Ham and Cheese Salad

1 cos lettuce, trimmed and
roughly torn
1 carton of salad cress, trimmed
2 peaches, stones removed and
cut into thin wedges
100g/4oz edam, rind removed
and cut into sticks
100g/4oz thick-sliced ham,
cut into sticks
warm crusty bread, to serve

FOR THE DRESSING
3 tbsp olive oil
1 tbsp white wine vinegar
1 tsp Dijon mustard
2 tbsp mayonnaise
1 tsp clear honey

Takes 25 minutes • Serves 4

1 Toss the lettuce, cress, peaches, cheese and thick-sliced ham together in a large salad bowl.
2 Whisk together the dressing ingredients and season to taste.
3 Toss the salad with the dressing just before serving. Serve with plenty of warm crusty bread.

• Per serving 286 kcalories, protein 12g, carbohydrate 7g, fat 23g, saturated fat 7g, fibre 3g, added sugar none, salt 1.63g

Buy a bottle of honey and mustard dressing
or mix up your own version.

Chicken Salad with Honey Dressing

450g/1lb new potatoes, scrubbed
and quartered lengthways
175g/6oz fine green beans, trimmed
6 rashers rindless streaky bacon
120g bag mixed salad leaves
4 roasted chicken breasts, skinned
and cut into chunks, or about
700g/1lb 9oz cooked chicken
ready-made honey and
mustard dressing

Takes 40 minutes • Serves 4

1 Cook the potatoes in salted boiling water for 8–10 minutes. Add the beans to the water and cook for a further 3 minutes until just tender. Drain, cool quickly under running cold water, then cool completely.
2 Meanwhile, fry or grill the bacon for 3–4 minutes until crispy. Allow to cool, then break into small pieces.
3 Scatter the salad leaves, potatoes and beans over a large serving plate. Toss the chicken with the dressing to taste, then spoon over the salad leaves. Scatter the crispy bacon over the salad and serve.

• Per serving 505 kcalories, protein 42g, carbohydrate 26g, fat 27g, saturated fat 5g, fibre 3g, added sugar 6g, salt 2.02g

An easy salad to get together and it's versatile too.
Try it with prawns instead of chicken.

Pesto, Chicken and Potato Salad

500g/1lb 2oz new
potatoes, unpeeled
350g/12oz skinned, cooked chicken
(about 3 breasts), cut into chunks
100g/4oz baby spinach leaves
2 tbsp pesto
juice of 1 small lemon
3 tbsp olive oil

Takes 25 minutes • Serves 4

1 Drop the potatoes into a pan of salted boiling water and boil for 15 minutes. Drain, then return them to the pan and roughly crush with a fork.
2 Tip the chunks of chicken into the pan and scatter in the spinach leaves. Mix gently, using a large spoon.
3 Mix the pesto, lemon juice and olive oil, then tip into the pan, season to taste and toss to coat everything in the dressing.

• Per serving 365 kcalories, protein 27g, carbohydrate 21g, fat 20g, saturated fat 5g, fibre 2g, added sugar none, salt 0.39g

Choose a bag with radicchio, frisée, watercress or rocket –
the bitter flavours are great with sweet red peppers.

Leaf Salad with Griddled Chicken

4 boneless skinless chicken breasts,
each cut into 7–8 slices
2 red peppers, seeded and
cut into strips
3 tbsp olive oil, plus extra
for tossing
juice of 1 lemon
142ml carton soured cream
200g bag mixed salad leaves

Takes 25 minutes • Serves 4

1 Heat a large griddle or frying pan. In a bowl, toss together the chicken, peppers, a little oil, some seasoning and a little of the lemon juice.
2 Cook the chicken and peppers in batches, in one layer in the hot pan for 5–8 minutes. Turn them halfway through until the chicken is cooked and the peppers are slightly charred. Allow to cool.
3 Mix together the remaining lemon juice and the soured cream. Whisk in the three tablespoons of oil and season. Tip the salad leaves into a bowl. Add the chicken and peppers, pour over the dressing, toss lightly and serve.

• Per serving 331 kcalories, protein 36g, carbohydrate 7g, fat 18g, saturated fat 6g, fibre 2g, added sugar none, salt 0.26g

Get everything ready and sizzle the bacon and
livers as guests sit down for a quick lunch or supper.

Warm Chicken Liver Salad

142g jar roasted peppers in olive oil,
drained and cut into strips
2 × 40g packs of lamb's lettuce
25g/1oz plain flour
400g/14oz chicken livers, trimmed
and thinly sliced
4 rashers streaky bacon,
coarsely chopped
2 tbsp olive oil
2 tsp red wine vinegar

Takes 15 minutes • Serves 4

1 Toss the strips of pepper with the lettuce
and divide into piles between four plates.
Season the flour and use it to coat the
chicken livers.
2 Heat a frying pan and add the chopped
bacon. Dry fry until crisp, then remove and
set aside on kitchen paper. Heat the oil
in the pan and fry the chicken livers for
30 seconds to 1 minute on each side.
Remove from the heat and stir in the red
wine vinegar.
3 Arrange the chicken livers on the lamb's
lettuce and peppers. Scatter over the bacon,
drizzle over the dressing from the pan,
season with black pepper and serve
immediately.

• Per serving 257 kcalories, protein 23g, carbohydrate
7g, fat 15g, saturated fat 4g, fibre 1g, added sugar
none, salt 1g

A French speciality – a toasted ham and cheese
sandwich that's perfect as a snack.

Croque Monsieur

2 thick slices crusty bread
butter, for spreading
2–3 slices wafer-thin ham
25g/1oz gruyère or cheddar, grated
4 tsp freshly grated parmesan
green salad, to serve

Takes 10 minutes • Serves 1

1 Preheat the grill. Butter the bread and make a sandwich with the ham and gruyère or cheddar. Press down firmly.
2 Spread butter over the top of the sandwich and sprinkle with half the parmesan, then toast under a moderate grill until the bread is crisp and the cheese browned.
3 Repeat on the other side. Cut in half and serve hot with a green salad.

• Per serving 533 kcalories, protein 25g, carbohydrate 51g, fat 27g, saturated fat 16g, fibre 2g, added sugar none, salt 2.97g

If you prefer, heat the beans in a pan
and grill the cheese-topped chips.

Tortilla Chips with Cheese and Salsa

2 tomatoes, quartered
½ small red onion, quartered
juice of ½ lime or lemon
4–5 drops Tabasco
2 tbsp tomato purée
150g bag tortilla chips
220g can refried beans
85g/3oz mature cheddar, grated
142ml carton soured cream,
to serve

Takes 10 minutes • Serves 2
(easily doubled)

1 Put the tomatoes, onion, lime or lemon juice and Tabasco in a food processor and whizz briefly until finely chopped. Stir in the tomato purée and season.
2 Divide the tortilla chips between two microwaveable plates. Spoon the beans into the centre, then top with the salsa.
3 Sprinkle the cheese over everything, then microwave on High, one plate at a time, for 2½ minutes. Serve with soured cream and extra Tabasco, if you like.

• Per serving 784 kcalories, protein 26g, carbohydrate 72g, fat 46g, saturated fat 17g, fibre 6g, added sugar none, salt 3.8g

A cheap and easy family supper.
Make a veggie version by omitting the ham.

Cheese and Onion Potato Wedges

4 baking potatoes, cut into
thick wedges
1 red pepper
bunch of spring onions
100g/4oz cheddar
100g/4oz wafer-thin ham
1 tsp paprika
200ml carton crème fraîche

Takes 30 minutes • Serves 4

1 Preheat the grill to high. Cook the potato wedges in a large pan of salted boiling water for 15 minutes until tender.
2 Meanwhile, seed and thinly slice the pepper, chop the spring onions and grate the cheese. Drain the potatoes well, then mix with the red pepper, spring onions and ham. Transfer to a heatproof dish. Season well and sprinkle with paprika. Grill for 3 minutes until golden brown.
3 Spoon over the crème fraîche, sprinkle with the cheese and grill for 2–3 minutes more, until the cheese has melted and the crème fraîche has made a sauce.

• Per serving 456 kcalories, protein 18g, carbohydrate 41g, fat 26g, saturated fat 14g, fibre 4g, added sugar none, salt 1.36g

These potatoes are cooked in the microwave for speed.
Vary the filling according to what's in the fridge.

Pizza Jackets

4 baking potatoes
2 tomatoes
2 × 150g balls mozzarella
4 small ham slices
4 fresh rosemary sprigs
olive oil, for drizzling

Takes 25 minutes • Serves 4

1 Wash the potatoes and prick them all over with a fork. Cook in the microwave on High for 10–12 minutes, turning halfway through, until cooked.

2 Preheat the grill. Slice each tomato and each mozzarella ball into six. Tear each ham slice into three strips. Cut three vertical slits in each potato and stuff each with a slice of cheese, ham and tomato. Tuck a rosemary sprig in the central slit.

3 Drizzle over a little oil and season. Grill for about 5 minutes until the cheese has melted.

• Per serving 421 kcalories, protein 28g, carbohydrate 32g, fat 21g, saturated fat 11g, fibre 3g, added sugar none, salt 2.36g

A rich alternative to everyday cauliflower cheese,
with a crisp almond topping.

Stilton Cauliflower Cheese

1 large cauliflower
50g/2oz blanched almonds

FOR THE SAUCE
25g/1oz butter
2 tbsp plain flour
300ml/½ pint milk
1 tsp dry mustard
85g/3oz stilton, plus 25g/1oz
extra for sprinkling

Takes 25 minutes • Serves 4

1 Divide the cauliflower into florets and discard all inedible parts. Steam for 10 minutes until just tender. Meanwhile, preheat the grill. Halve the almonds lengthways and toast for 4–5 minutes, turning halfway through, until browned.
2 To make the sauce, put all the ingredients (including the cheese) in a wide pan and season. Heat gently and bring to the boil, whisking all the time, then simmer for 2 minutes, stirring constantly. Season carefully (go easy on the salt).
3 Put the cauliflower in a wide heatproof serving dish and sprinkle with half the toasted almonds. Top with the sauce, remaining almonds and the rest of the cheese. Grill for 5–10 minutes until the cheese is brown and bubbling.

• Per serving 366 kcalories, protein 17g, carbohydrate 17g, fat 26g, saturated fat 11g, fibre 4g, added sugar none, salt 1.1g

Choose large flat mushrooms for
stuffing with cheesy mashed potato.

Cheese-stuffed Mushrooms

4 large or 8 medium flat mushrooms
3 tbsp olive oil
2 large floury potatoes
4 or 8 rashers rindless smoked
streaky bacon
125g pack soft cheese with garlic
and herbs

Takes 25 minutes • Serves 4

1 Preheat the oven to 200°C/Gas 6/fan
oven 180°C. Wipe the mushrooms clean.
Put them in an ovenproof dish, drizzle with
the oil and bake for 15–20 minutes.
2 Meanwhile, cut the potatoes into small
cubes, then cook in a pan of salted boiling
water for 8–10 minutes until just tender.
3 Heat a frying pan and dry fry the bacon
until crisp. Drain the potatoes, return to the
pan and spoon in the cheese. Mix together
lightly, then season. Pile the mixture on top
of the mushrooms and top with the bacon.

• Per serving 392 kcalories, protein 14g, carbohydrate
22g, fat 28g, saturated fat 5g, fibre 3g, added sugar
none, salt 1.58g

Cut the slices from a nice loaf,
a few days old, for the best texture.

Cheese and Mustard Bake

175g/6oz mature cheddar, finely grated
2 tsp Dijon or English mustard
850ml/1½ pints semi-skimmed milk
25g/1oz butter, at room temperature
5 thick slices white bread
3 eggs
4 rashers rindless streaky bacon
Worcestershire sauce, to serve

Takes 50 minutes • Serves 4

1 Preheat the oven to 180°C/Gas 4/fan oven 160°C. Mix together most of the cheese, the mustard and three tablespoons of the milk. Season. Butter the bread. Spread each slice with the cheese mixture. Cut each slice into four triangles. Butter a 2.25 litre/4 pint ovenproof dish and arrange the bread in the dish with the points uppermost.
2 Beat together the remaining milk and eggs, and season. Pour the liquid over the bread. Sprinkle with the remaining cheese. Bake for 35 minutes until risen and golden.
3 Meanwhile, preheat the grill. Grill the bacon for 8–10 minutes until crispy, turning halfway through. Break into pieces and scatter over the pudding. Sprinkle with a little Worcestershire sauce and serve immediately.

• Per serving 569 kcalories, protein 31g, carbohydrate 36g, fat 35g, saturated fat 19g, fibre 1g, added sugar none, salt 2.94g

The addition of potatoes, leeks and prawns
makes a meal of scrambled eggs.

Spanish-style Scrambled Eggs

2 medium potatoes
1 leek
3 tbsp olive oil
1 garlic clove, chopped
4 eggs
3 tbsp milk
100g/4oz peeled prawns,
defrosted if frozen
Tabasco, for sprinkling (optional)

Takes 25 minutes • Serves 2

1 Cut the potatoes into small cubes (no need to peel). Slice the leek finely. Heat the oil in a frying pan, add the potatoes and fry for about 10 minutes, until they are just tender.
2 Stir in the leek and garlic and cook for a further 5 minutes, until softened.
3 Beat together the eggs, milk and seasoning. Stir the prawns into the pan. Add the eggs and cook gently, stirring, until scrambled. Serve piping hot, sprinkled with Tabasco.

• Per serving 468 kcalories, protein 28g, carbohydrate 25g, fat 29g, saturated fat 6g, fibre 3g, added sugar none, salt 1.16g

A delicious combination of tender asparagus,
creamy sauce and crispy crumbs.

Asparagus Carbonara

knob of butter
1 small onion, chopped
2 garlic cloves, finely chopped
225g/8oz ham, cut into chunks
600g/1lb 5oz asparagus spears
2 eggs
142ml carton single cream
4 tbsp freshly grated parmesan
85g/3oz fresh white breadcrumbs
2 tbsp olive oil
2 tbsp finely chopped fresh parsley

Takes 30 minutes • Serves 4

1 Melt the butter in a small frying pan, then cook the onion, garlic and ham for 5–10 minutes until golden. Meanwhile, cook the asparagus in a pan of salted boiling water for 3–4 minutes until just tender. Drain.
2 Whisk together the eggs, cream and three tablespoons of the parmesan. Stir in the onion mixture and season. In a separate bowl, mix together the breadcrumbs, olive oil, parsley and remaining parmesan.
3 Preheat the grill. Toss the asparagus with the cream mixture. Tip into a gratin dish and sprinkle over the breadcrumb mixture. Grill for 2–3 minutes, until the breadcrumbs are golden and the carbonara sauce is hot.

• Per serving 381 kcalories, protein 25g, carbohydrate 21g, fat 22g, saturated fat 9g, fibre 4g, added sugar none, salt 2.07g

You could use leftover cooked pasta in this recipe.
Be sure to drain the spinach well.

Pasta and Spinach Tortilla

85g/3oz pasta shells
450g/1lb fresh spinach
8 eggs
100g/4oz mature cheddar,
coarsely grated
225g/8oz cherry tomatoes, halved
1 tbsp olive oil

Takes 25 minutes • Serves 4

1 Cook the pasta in salted boiling water. drain. Wash the spinach well, then put in the pan with just the water that clings to it and a little salt. Put over a medium heat. When the spinach starts to steam, cover and cook for 3–4 minutes until just wilted. Drain the spinach well, then roughly chop. Mix into the pasta.

2 Lightly beat the eggs and mix into the pasta with three-quarters of the cheese and the tomatoes. Season. Preheat the grill. Heat one tablespoon of olive oil in a large frying pan and cook the pasta and egg mixture for 8–10 minutes, until almost set.

3 Sprinkle the omelette with the remaining cheese, then grill to brown the top. Serve warm or cold cut into wedges.

• Per serving 361 kcalories, protein 25g, carbohydrate 19g, fat 21g, saturated fat 9g, fibre 4g, added sugar none, salt 1.2g

You could use cooked bacon instead of ham and gruyère in place of cheddar.

Florentine Egg Grill

225g/8oz frozen leaf spinach, thawed
freshly grated nutmeg
knob of butter
2 ham slices, cut into thin strips
2 eggs
2 tbsp single or double cream
85g/3oz cheddar, grated

Takes 25 minutes • Serves 2

1 Drain the thawed spinach well. Tip into a bowl and stir in a little nutmeg, a knob of butter and the ham. Season. Form into two mounds on the base of a shallow, buttered ovenproof dish.

2 Preheat the grill to high. Poach the eggs in a pan half full of lightly salted water until just set.

3 Lift out with a slotted spoon, drain well and place on the spinach cakes. Drizzle with the cream and sprinkle with the cheese. Grill until golden brown.

• Per serving 368 kcalories, protein 26g, carbohydrate 3g, fat 28g, saturated fat 15g, fibre 2g, added sugar none, salt 2.12g

If you can't find fresh horseradish,
add creamed horseradish to taste. Serve with toast.

Mackerel and Horseradish Pâté

225g/8oz smoked mackerel fillets, skinned and boned
3 tbsp freshly grated horseradish
100g/4oz ricotta cheese
4–5 tsp fresh lemon juice
1 tsp fennel seeds, crushed
2 tbsp melted butter
bay leaves and pink or green peppercorns, to garnish
toast or rye bread, to serve

Takes 25 minutes, plus chilling • Serves 4

1 In a food processor, blend the fish, horseradish, ricotta, four teaspoons of lemon juice, fennel and pepper to a smooth paste.
2 Taste and add more lemon juice, if necessary. Spoon into a serving bowl and drizzle over the butter.
3 Garnish with bay leaves and peppercorns and chill for 1 hour before serving with the toast.

• Per serving 283 kcalories, protein 13g, carbohydrate 3g, fat 25g, saturated fat 9g, fibre 1g, added sugar none, salt 1.17g

Frittata is an Italian omelette. Use cheaper
smoked salmon trimmings for this light supper.

Smoked Salmon Frittata

500g/1lb 2oz new potatoes,
thickly sliced
200g pack smoked salmon
8 large eggs
2 tbsp chopped fresh dill
100g/4oz frozen petits pois
3 tbsp olive oil

Takes 40 minutes • Serves 4

1 Cook the potatoes in salted boiling water
until just tender, about 10 minutes. Drain
and leave to cool slightly. Cut the salmon
into wide strips. Crack the eggs into a bowl,
beat with a fork until foamy, then stir in the
smoked salmon, dill and peas, and season.
Finally, stir in the potatoes.
2 Heat three tablespoons of olive oil in a
large non-stick frying pan and carefully pour
in the egg mixture. Cook over a fairly low
heat for 10–15 minutes, until the egg is
starting to set just under the surface.
3 Put a plate over the pan and invert the
frittata on to it. Slide it back into the pan and
cook for a further 5 minutes to brown the
underside. Slide on to a plate and cool for
5 minutes before cutting into wedges.

• Per serving 423 kcalories, protein 31g, carbohydrate
22g, fat 24g, saturated fat 5g, fibre 3g, added sugar
none, salt 3.15g

This spicy rice mix is a favourite
snack in Indonesia.

Nasi Goreng

350g/12oz long grain rice
2 tbsp sunflower oil, plus 1 tsp
2 garlic cloves, roughly chopped
450g/1lb boneless skinless chicken
breasts or thighs, cut into chunks
1 red pepper, seeded and diced
1 tbsp curry paste or powder
bunch of spring onions, thinly sliced
2 tbsp soy sauce, plus
extra to serve
2 eggs
50g/2oz roasted peanuts,
roughly chopped
4 tbsp roughly chopped
fresh coriander

Takes 35 minutes • Serves 4

1 Cook the rice in salted boiling water for 12–15 minutes. Drain well. Meanwhile, heat the two tablespoons of oil in a wok or large frying pan.
2 Fry the garlic, chicken and pepper for 10 minutes, stirring, until golden. Add the curry paste or powder and cook for 1 minute. Stir in the rice and spring onions and cook for 5 minutes until piping hot. Stir in the two tablespoons of soy sauce.
3 Push the rice to one side of the pan. Pour the remaining teaspoon of oil in the space, crack in the eggs and lightly scramble them. Mix into the rice. Sprinkle over the peanuts, coriander and extra soy sauce. Serve immediately.

• Per serving 625 kcalories, protein 34g, carbohydrate 73g, fat 24g, saturated fat 2g, fibre 4g, added sugar none, salt 2.23g

Make these ahead and store in the
fridge, covered with cling film.

Spicy Lamb Burgers

1 onion, roughly chopped
2.5cm/1in piece of fresh root ginger,
peeled and chopped
2 garlic cloves, roughly chopped
a bunch of fresh coriander or parsley
2 tsp each of ground cumin and
ground coriander
1 tsp ground cinnamon
100g/4oz ready-to-eat dried
apricots, finely chopped
700g/1lb 9oz lean minced lamb
oil, for brushing

TO SERVE
6 large buns, such as ciabatta rolls
2 tsp harissa paste (available from
large supermarkets) or chilli paste
8 tbsp mayonnaise
a few lettuce leaves, and tomato and
cucumber slices

Takes 30 minutes • Serves 6

1 Whizz the onion, ginger, garlic and
coriander or parsley (stems too) in a food
processor until finely chopped. Add the
spices, apricots, lamb, and plenty of
seasoning, then pulse until just mixed.
2 Shape into six burgers, brush lightly with
oil and cook on a hot griddle, or under the
grill, for 4–5 minutes on each side.
3 Split and toast the buns. Swirl the harissa
or chilli paste into the mayonnaise. Serve the
burgers, lettuce, tomato and cucumber in
the buns, with the mayonnaise on the side.

• Per serving 497 kcalories, protein 30g, carbohydrate
34g, fat 28g, saturated fat 8g, fibre 2g, added sugar
none, salt 1.21g

Look for stir fry sauces and
no-need-to-cook noodles in the supermarket.

Steak and Noodle Stir Fry

225g/8oz rump steak
225g/8oz pak choi (Chinese greens)
1 red pepper, seeded
2 tbsp sunflower oil
100–120g sachet stir fry sauce
2 × 150g packs no-cook noodles

Takes 10 minutes • Serves 2

1 Trim any visible fat from the steak, then slice into thin strips. Cut each head of pak choi into four lengthways. Dice the pepper into small squares.

2 Heat two tablespoons of sunflower oil in a pan. Add the pepper and fry quickly for 1 minute. Add the beef and fry until browned all over. Add the pak choi and cook briefly until starting to wilt.

3 Tip in the stir fry sauce and two table-spoons of water and stir. Bring to the boil, then add the noodles and warm through, loosening them until they are all coated in sauce. Serve immediately.

• Per serving 499 kcalories, protein 32g, carbohydrate 53.8g, fat 18.9g, saturated fat 3.1g, fibre 3.8g, added sugar 1.6g, salt 2.52g

A quick, fresh-tasting dish,
spiked with chilli.

Mozzarella Pasta with Olives

350g/12oz penne or rigatoni
1 small red onion, finely chopped
1 red chilli, seeded and
finely chopped
450g/1lb ripe tomatoes, chopped
6 tbsp olive oil
225g/8oz buffalo
mozzarella, chopped
handful of small fresh basil or
mint leaves
100g/4oz black olives

Takes 25 minutes • Serves 4

1 In a large pan of salted boiling water, cook the pasta for 10–12 minutes, stirring from time to time.

2 Meanwhile, mix together the onion, chilli and tomatoes in a large bowl. Season well, then stir in the olive oil.

3 Drain the pasta and tip it into the tomato mixture with the mozzarella, basil and olives. Stir well and serve.

• Per serving 650 kcalories, protein 24g, carbohydrate 71g, fat 32g, saturated fat 10g, fibre 5g, added sugar none, salt 2.26g

These tiny tomatoes taste extra sweet when roasted,
and are a contrast to the salty cheese.

Spaghetti with Cherry Tomatoes

500g/1lb 2oz cherry tomatoes
3 tbsp olive oil
400g/14oz spaghetti
250g/9oz Greek feta
generous handful fresh flatleaf
parsley (or a supermarket pack)
a handful of black olives
freshly grated parmesan, to serve

Takes 25 minutes • Serves 4

1 Preheat the oven to 200°C/Gas 6/fan oven 180°C. Tip the tomatoes into a shallow ovenproof dish, drizzle over three tablespoons of olive oil, and season. Roast for 15 minutes until slightly scorched.
2 Cook the spaghetti in plenty of salted boiling water for 10–12 minutes, until just tender. Meanwhile, cut the feta into cubes and roughly chop the parsley.
3 Drain the pasta, then return to the pan. Add the roasted tomatoes, along with their pan juices, the feta, olives and parsley. Toss together until well mixed, then serve with freshly grated parmesan for sprinkling.

• Per serving 530 kcalories, protein 23g, carbohydrate 79g, fat 16g, saturated fat 8g, fibre 5g, added sugar none, salt 3.02g

A creamy vegetarian pasta that's perfect when
you fancy some comfort food.

Penne with Blue Cheese

350g/12oz penne
225g/8oz frozen leaf spinach
85g/3oz Danish blue, crumbled
pinch of chilli flakes
250g tub mascarpone
25g/1oz freshly grated parmesan
green salad, to serve

Takes 20 minutes • Serves 4

1 Bring a large pan of salted water to the boil. Add the pasta and cook for 10–12 minutes until tender, adding the spinach to the pan for the last 3 minutes of cooking time. Drain.
2 Tip the pasta and spinach into a shallow heatproof dish along with the Danish blue, a pinch of chilli flakes and plenty of black pepper.
3 Dot spoonfuls of the mascarpone over the top of the pasta mixture. Sprinkle with the parmesan and grill for 5 minutes, until the mascarpone melts into a sauce and the parmesan turns golden. Serve with a green salad.

• Per serving 698 kcalories, protein 21g, carbohydrate 70g, fat 39g, saturated fat 24g, fibre 4g, added sugar none, salt 1.06g

Mushrooms add a deliciously nutty flavour
and juicy texture to this veggie-friendly pasta.

Tagliatelle with Goat's Cheese

250g/9oz chestnut mushrooms
1 small onion
2 garlic cloves
175g/6oz tagliatelle
25g/1oz butter
1 tbsp olive oil, plus
extra for drizzling
100g/4oz firm goat's cheese,
such as Capricorn
freshly shaved parmesan,
for serving

Takes 20 minutes • Serves 2
(easily doubled)

1 Slice the mushrooms and finely chop the onion and garlic. Cook the pasta in plenty of salted boiling water according to the packet instructions.

2 Heat the butter and oil in a frying pan until the butter is melted. Add the onion and cook until golden, about 3–4 minutes. Stir in the garlic and mushrooms and cook, stirring, until the mushrooms are golden brown.

3 Drain the pasta, reserving four tablespoons of the pasta water. Return the pasta to its pan with the reserved water and stir in the mushroom mixture. Roughly break the goat's cheese into pieces and gently stir it into the pasta so it starts to melt. Serve sprinkled with black pepper, a drizzle of olive oil and a few shavings of parmesan.

• Per serving 598 kcalories, protein 20g, carbohydrate 71g, fat 28g, saturated fat 8g, fibre 5g, added sugar none, salt 0.88g

Tube-shaped pasta shapes work best in this recipe, as the sauce gets trapped inside and clings to their ridged surfaces.

Stilton and Broccoli Pasta

350g/12oz penne or rigatoni
350g/12oz broccoli, cut into florets
140g/5oz stilton
6 rashers rindless streaky bacon
200ml carton crème fraîche

Takes 25 minutes • Serves 4

1 Cook the pasta in a large pan of salted boiling water for 5 minutes. Add the broccoli, return the water to the boil and cook for a further 5–7 minutes, until the pasta and broccoli are just tender.

2 While the pasta is cooking, crumble the stilton into a small bowl. Grill the bacon until crispy, then cut into pieces. Drain the pasta, reserving a few tablespoons of the cooking water. Return the pasta and reserved water to the pan.

3 Stir in the crumbled stilton, crème fraîche and plenty of freshly ground black pepper. Stir gently until the cheese starts to melt into the sauce. Serve sprinkled with the bacon pieces and ground black pepper.

• Per serving 736 kcalories, protein 30g, carbohydrate 70g, fat 39g, saturated fat 20g, fibre 5g, added sugar none, salt 2.2g

You'll find most of these ingredients in your storecupboard.
Vary the green vegetables as you like.

Broccoli and Spaghetti Bake

1 tbsp olive oil
1 onion, chopped
400g can chopped tomatoes
25g/1oz butter
25g/1oz plain flour
600ml/1 pint semi-skimmed milk
ground nutmeg
300g/10oz broken-up spaghetti
300g/10oz broccoli, cut into florets
100g/4oz mature cheddar, grated

Takes 45 minutes • Serves 4

1 Heat the oil in a small pan and fry the onion until soft. Stir in the tomatoes and season. Boil for 10 minutes, stirring until thickened. Meanwhile, put the butter, flour and milk into a pan. Bring to the boil, whisking until thick and smooth.
2 Cook the spaghetti in salted boiling water for 8 minutes, then add the broccoli and cook for 4 more minutes. Preheat the grill. Stir most of the cheese into the white sauce.
3 Drain the pasta, mix with the cheese sauce and spoon half into a 1.7 litre/3 pint dish. Spoon the tomato sauce over. Cover with the rest of the pasta and sprinkle with the remaining cheese. Grill for 5–8 minutes until golden.

• Per serving 574 kcalories, protein 26g, carbohydrate 75g, fat 21g, saturated fat 11g, fibre 6g, added sugar none, salt 0.98g

Salty anchovies and capers add a piquant
flavour to peppery watercress sauce.

Linguine with Watercress Sauce

300g/10oz linguine or spaghetti
1 garlic clove, peeled
6 anchovies in oil, drained
1 tbsp capers, drained and
well rinsed
50g/2oz watercress
6 tbsp olive oil

Takes 20 minutes • Serves 4

1 Cook the pasta in a large pan of salted
boiling water according to the packet
instructions, until the pasta is tender.
2 Meanwhile, put the garlic, anchovies and
capers in a food processor and whizz until
well blended. Add the watercress and whizz
again until the mixture is finely chopped. With
the motor running, drizzle in the olive oil to
make a soft paste.
3 Mix four tablespoons of the pasta
cooking water into the watercress sauce,
then season to taste. Drain the pasta and
return to the pan. Stir in the sauce and
divide between four bowls. Grind over plenty
of black pepper and serve immediately.

• Per serving 422 kcalories, protein 11g, carbohydrate
56g, fat 19g, saturated fat 3g, fibre 3g, added sugar
none, salt 0.53g

Reduce the calories by using a
low-fat soft cheese with garlic and herbs.

Creamy Salmon Pasta

300g/10oz penne or rigatoni
350g/12oz broccoli,
cut into small florets
300g/10oz boneless skinless salmon
fillet (about 2 fillets)
150g packet soft cheese with
garlic and herbs
142ml carton single cream
2 tbsp sun-dried tomato paste

Takes 20 minutes • Serves 4

1 Cook the pasta according to the packet instructions, adding the broccoli for the last 3 minutes of cooking. Meanwhile, put the salmon in a frying pan, season and just cover with water. Bring to the boil, then simmer, covered, for 6 minutes until the flesh flakes easily with a fork. Using a slotted spoon, transfer to a plate and keep warm.
2 Mix the soft cheese with the cream and sun-dried tomato paste to make a smooth sauce. Season to taste.
3 Drain the pasta and broccoli, then tip back into the pan. Pour in the sauce and stir well. Flake the salmon into large chunks and gently mix into the pasta. Transfer to a warm serving bowl, season with black pepper and serve.

• Per serving 586 kcalories, protein 33g, carbohydrate 61g, fat 25g, saturated fat 6g, fibre 5g, added sugar none, salt 0.53g

Try this easy, no-cook sauce when
you see dressed crab on the fish counter.

Tagliatelle with Crab and Salsa

225g/8oz tagliatelle
4 tbsp olive oil
1 tbsp fresh lemon juice
3 tbsp chopped fresh parsley
1 small red onion, finely chopped
3 ripe tomatoes, seeded
and chopped
170g can white crabmeat, drained,
or 175g/6oz fresh or frozen crab
green salad, to serve

Takes 20 minutes • Serves 2

1 Cook the tagliatelle in a large pan of
salted boiling water for 10–12 minutes
(or according to the pack instructions).
2 Whisk together the olive oil and lemon
juice, season and stir in the parsley.
3 Drain the pasta and toss with the olive
oil mixture, red onion, tomatoes and crab.
Serve straightaway with a green salad.

• Per serving 634 kcalories, protein 26g, carbohydrate
82g, fat 25g, saturated fat 3g, fibre 5g, added sugar
none, salt 1.02g

Use raw prawns for special occasions,
but frozen ones will do for a midweek supper.

Prawn Tagliatelle with Lemon

350g/12oz tagliatelle
225g/8oz fine green beans,
trimmed and halved
85g/3oz butter
2 tbsp olive oil
finely grated zest and juice of
1 small lemon
300g/10oz raw peeled king prawns
2 tbsp chopped fresh dill, to serve

Takes 15 minutes • Serves 4

1 Cook the pasta according to the packet instructions. Three minutes before the end of the cooking time, throw in the green beans.
2 While the pasta is cooking, melt the butter in a small pan and stir in the olive oil, lemon zest and juice, and the prawns. Cook over a low heat for 3–4 minutes, stirring occasionally, until the prawns turn pink. Season to taste.
3 Drain the pasta and beans, reserving about four tablespoons of the cooking liquid. Toss with the prawn sauce and add enough cooking liquid to make a sauce. Serve sprinkled with the fresh dill.

• Per serving 581 kcalories, protein 25g, carbohydrate 68g, fat 25g, saturated fat 12g, fibre 4g, added sugar none, salt 0.79g

Try adding prawns instead of bacon,
and chopped fresh dill instead of parsley.

Pasta and Cod Bake

350g/12oz pasta shells
6 streaky bacon rashers,
cut into strips
350g carton fresh Napoletana sauce
(from the chiller cabinet)
finely grated zest of 1 lemon
500g/1lb 2oz cod fillets, cut into
4cm/1½in pieces
4 tbsp crème fraîche
3 tbsp chopped fresh parsley
50g/2oz freshly grated cheddar
or parmesan

Takes 25 minutes • Serves 4

1 Cook the pasta in salted boiling water for 10–12 minutes until tender, stirring once.
2 Dry fry the bacon for 5 minutes until crisp. Add the Napoletana sauce and stir well until it just starts to bubble. Stir in the lemon zest and add the cod. Cover and cook for 4 minutes until the fish is just cooked.
3 Preheat the grill to high. Drain the pasta and stir into the sauce with the crème fraîche and parsley. Season. Spoon into a shallow heatproof dish. Sprinkle over the cheese and grill until melted and golden.

• Per serving 651 kcalories, protein 44g, carbohydrate 72g, fat 23g, saturated fat 10g, fibre 4g, added sugar 2g, salt 3.24g

This all-in-one sauce gives perfect results.
Whisk until the mixture boils, then simmer for 5 minutes.

Pasta and Haddock Gratin

350g/12oz penne or rigatoni
175g/6oz frozen leaf spinach
25g/1oz butter
25g/1oz plain flour
600ml/1 pint milk
450g/1lb skinless haddock or cod
fillet, cut into chunks
175g/6oz mature cheddar, grated
2 tomatoes, sliced

Takes 30 minutes • Serves 4

1 Cook the pasta in salted boiling water for about 12 minutes. Add the spinach for the last 3 minutes of cooking time.
2 Meanwhile, whisk the butter, flour and milk in a large pan until the mixture comes to the boil. Reduce the heat, add the fish and simmer for 5 minutes or until the fish is just cooked. Remove from the heat and stir in three-quarters of the cheese. Season to taste.
3 Preheat the grill. Drain the pasta and stir into the sauce. Pour into a 1.2–1.4 litre/2–2½ pint shallow ovenproof dish. Put the tomatoes on top and sprinkle with the remaining cheese. Grill for 5–7 minutes until golden.

• Per serving 751 kcalories, protein 48g, carbohydrate 80g, fat 29g, saturated fat 17g, fibre 4g, added sugar none, salt 1.61g

Try to use dry-cure bacon as it is better for
dry frying and will give a crisper finish.

Spinach, Bacon and Pine Nut Pasta

finely grated zest of 1 lemon,
plus 2 tbsp juice
3 tbsp olive oil, plus extra
for drizzling
300g/10oz pasta, such
as pappardelle
4 rashers streaky bacon,
cut into strips
50g/2oz pine nuts
225g bag baby leaf spinach,
thick stalks removed

Takes 25 minutes • Serves 4
(easily halved)

1 Mix the lemon zest and juice with the olive oil. Season and set aside. Cook the pasta in a large pan of salted boiling water for 10–12 minutes.
2 Meanwhile, heat a frying pan and dry fry the bacon until golden. Tip in the pine nuts and cook with the bacon until toasted golden.
3 Drain the pasta, return to the hot pan and tip in the spinach leaves, stirring gently until wilted. Toss in the bacon, pine nuts and the lemon dressing. Season to taste, then serve drizzled with a little olive oil and sprinkled with black pepper.

• Per serving 495 kcalories, protein 16g, carbohydrate 59g, fat 23g, saturated fat 4g, fibre 4g, added sugar none, salt 0.86g

Instead of a sauce this light, summery pasta
has a mustardy vinaigrette dressing.

Pasta with Asparagus and Mustard

250g/9oz spaghetti
300g/10oz unsmoked back bacon,
rind removed
1 tbsp olive oil
250g/9oz asparagus, cut into
2.5cm/1in pieces
250g/9oz cherry tomatoes, halved
50g/2oz parmesan shavings
(use a potato peeler)

FOR THE DRESSING
5 tbsp olive oil
1½ tbsp white wine vinegar
2 tsp Dijon mustard

Takes 25 minutes • Serves 4

1 To make the dressing, put all the ingredients in a bowl and whisk until creamy. Season to taste, then set aside. Break the spaghetti into 7.5cm/3in pieces and cook in salted boiling water for 10–12 minutes, until just tender.

2 Cut the bacon into strips. Heat the oil in a large frying pan and fry the bacon for 5–6 minutes. Drain all but one tablespoon of the fat. Add the asparagus and fry for 3–4 minutes. Add the tomatoes and cook for 2 minutes.

3 Drain the pasta and tip into a serving bowl. Mix in the bacon and asparagus mixture and the mustard dressing. Top with parmesan shavings. Serve warm or cold with extra black pepper.

• Per serving 610 kcalories, protein 27g, carbohydrate 50g, fat 35g, saturated fat 10g, fibre 4g, added sugar none, salt 3.5g

Tzatziki, a cucumber and mint dip from Greece,
adds a refreshing kick to this dish.

Summer Garden Spaghetti

1 tbsp olive oil
225g/8oz smoked streaky
bacon, chopped
350g/12oz spaghetti
250g/9oz runner beans,
sliced diagonally
250g/9oz cherry tomatoes, halved
170g carton tzatziki

Takes 25 minutes • Serves 4
(easily halved)

1 Heat the oil in a frying pan, add the bacon and fry for about 10 minutes, stirring occasionally, until crisp.

2 Meanwhile, bring a large pan of salted water to the boil, add the spaghetti, stir once and cook at a rolling boil for 6 minutes. Stir in the beans and cook for 6 minutes more until tender.

3 Drain the pasta and beans and return to the pan with the bacon and cooking juices, the tomatoes and tzatziki. Toss together well, and season with plenty of black pepper. Serve warm.

• Per serving 515 kcalories, protein 22g, carbohydrate 70g, fat 19g, saturated fat 7g, fibre 5g, added sugar 5g, salt 2.02g

If you can't find orecchiette (literally, 'little ears') pasta, so-called because of their curved shape, substitute another shape.

Pasta with Bacon and Peas

300g/10oz pasta shapes, such as orecchiette
225g/8oz frozen peas
1 tbsp olive oil
1 onion, chopped
4 back bacon rashers, cut into strips
100ml/3½fl oz crème fraîche
fresh country bread and green salad, to serve

Takes 20 minutes • Serves 4

1 Cook the pasta in salted boiling water for 12 minutes, adding the frozen peas for the last 3 minutes of cooking.
2 Meanwhile, heat the oil in a frying pan, then cook the onion for 2–3 minutes until starting to brown. Add the bacon and cook over a high heat, stirring, until both the bacon and onion are golden and crisp.
3 Drain the pasta and toss with the onion and bacon. Stir in the crème fraîche. Season. Serve piping hot with fresh country bread and a simple green salad.

• Per serving 461 kcalories, protein 17g, carbohydrate 65g, fat 17g, saturated fat 7g, fibre 5g, added sugar none, salt 1.07g

Instead of courgettes, you could use a
200g pack of prepared stir-fry vegetables instead.

Ham and Courgette Tagliatelle

400g/14oz dried tagliatelle
3 tbsp olive oil
1 plump garlic clove, halved and
thinly sliced
4 courgettes, very thinly sliced
175g/6oz wafer-thin ham,
cut into thin strips
3 tbsp pesto

Takes 25 minutes • Serves 4

1 Cook the tagliatelle in salted boiling water for 8–10 minutes until just tender.
2 Meanwhile, heat the oil in a large pan or wok. Add the garlic slices and the courgettes, and fry over a high heat for about 3 minutes until soft and lightly browned. (You may need to do this in two batches.) Add the ham and toss together until heated through.
3 Drain the pasta well, add to the courgettes with the pesto, and season to taste. Toss well and serve.

• Per serving 555 kcalories, protein 24g, carbohydrate 77g, fat 19g, saturated fat 5g, fibre 4g, added sugar none, salt 1.31g

Using cartons of ready-made sauce saves time and effort.
Look for them in supermarket chiller cabinets.

Fusilli with Turkey and Mushrooms

1 tbsp olive oil
1 onion, sliced
1 red pepper, seeded and chopped
450g/1lb turkey fillet,
cut into chunks
350g/12oz fusilli
300g–350g carton wild mushroom
sauce, made up to
600ml/1 pint with milk
225g/8oz slice of ham,
cut into chunks
225g/8oz frozen leaf spinach
freshly grated nutmeg
100g/4oz mature cheddar, grated

Takes 25 minutes • Serves 6

1 Heat the oil in a large pan, then cook the onion and pepper for 5 minutes. Add the turkey and cook for another 5 minutes, stirring occasionally. Cook the pasta in salted boiling water for about 8–10 minutes until just tender. Drain well.

2 Preheat the grill to hot. Add the wild mushroom sauce mix to the turkey in the pan and bring to the boil, then stir in the pasta, ham and frozen spinach.

3 Season and add nutmeg to taste. Simmer for 5 minutes until piping hot. Spoon into a shallow heatproof dish, sprinkle with the cheese and grill until brown.

• Per serving 501 kcalories, protein 40g, carbohydrate 51g, fat 17g, saturated fat 7g, fibre 3g, added sugar none, salt 2.54g

Tuna and bacon may seem an odd
combination but they taste good together.

Stir-fried Tuna Rice

350g/12oz long grain rice
8 rashers rindless streaky bacon,
roughly chopped
2 tbsp vegetable oil
225g/8oz frozen peas, thawed
200g can tuna, drained
2–3 tbsp soy sauce, plus extra
to serve

Takes 30 minutes • Serves 4

1 Cook the rice, following the instructions on the packet, then set aside to cool slightly.
2 Heat a wok until hot. Add the bacon and stir fry for 2 minutes until crispy and browned. Remove from the wok and set aside.
3 Heat the oil in the wok and stir fry the rice for 2 minutes. Add the peas and tuna and stir fry over a high heat for 2–3 minutes. Add the soy sauce and crispy bacon and cook for a further 1 minute. Serve immediately, with extra soy sauce, if liked.

• Per serving 552 kcalories, protein 25g, carbohydrate 81g, fat 17g, saturated fat 5g, fibre 3g, added sugar none, salt 2.98g

Spanish chorizo sausages are perfect for this dish, or use one of the many brands of spicy sausages in supermarkets.

Spicy Sausage Rice

2 tbsp olive oil
4 spicy sausages, sliced
1 onion, sliced
300g/10oz risotto rice
190g jar of sun-dried tomato pasta sauce
1 litre/1¾ pints vegetable stock

Takes 30 minutes • Serves 4

1 Heat the oil in a heavy-based pan, then fry the sausages for 10 minutes until cooked through. Remove from the pan. Add the onion and cook for 7 minutes, stirring often, until softened. Stir in the rice and cook for 2 minutes, until the grains glisten.

2 Add the pasta sauce and stock, stir and bring to the boil. Reduce the heat and simmer, covered, for 12–15 minutes, stirring occasionally, until the rice has a creamy texture.

3 Stir the sausages into the rice. Remove from the heat and season with black pepper. Sprinkle with salt, if necessary, then stir and serve.

• Per serving 488 kcalories, protein 16g, carbohydrate 69g, fat 19g, saturated fat 5g, fibre 2g, added sugar 2g, salt 2.32g

No crackers? Crush a good handful of cornflakes
to make an equally quick and simple coating.

Parmesan Chicken

4 boneless skinless chicken breasts
juice of 1 small lemon
1 egg
4 cream crackers
50g/2oz parmesan, finely grated
2 tbsp oil
4 heaped tbsp crème fraîche
4 tsp sweet chilli dipping sauce
crisp salad and new potatoes,
to serve

Takes 30 minutes • Serves 4

1 Separate the chicken into breast and fillet pieces. Season all the pieces with lemon juice, salt and pepper. Beat the egg on a plate. Put the crackers in a bag and crush into crumbs, then mix with the parmesan on another plate.
2 Dip the chicken in the egg, then the cracker mixture, pressing it on evenly. Heat the oil in a large pan and fry the chicken on each side for 4–5 minutes, until well browned and crisp.
3 Transfer the chicken to serving plates, spoon some crème fraîche onto each plate and drizzle over the chilli sauce. Serve with a crisp salad and new potatoes.

• Per serving 345 kcalories, protein 32g, carbohydrate 7g, fat 21g, saturated fat 9g, fibre trace, added sugar none, salt 0.78g

Cook potato wedges, tossed in oil, for 45 minutes
in the oven, above the chicken.

Crunchy Almond Chicken

4 boneless skinless chicken
breasts, 140g/5oz each
100g/4oz stilton or other blue
cheese, crumbled
olive oil, for brushing
50g packet mixed nuts, chopped
2 tbsp chopped fresh parsley
4 tbsp cranberry sauce
chunky chips, to serve

Takes 50 minutes • Serves 4

1 Preheat the oven to 190°C/Gas 5/fan
oven 170°C from cold. Slit a pocket in each
chicken breast and stuff with the cheese.
Put in a shallow ovenproof dish, brush lightly
with oil and season.
2 Mix the nuts and parsley, then press on
to the chicken and bake, uncovered, for
25 minutes until golden and cooked through.
3 Gently heat the cranberry sauce in a
small pan. Serve the chicken with the sauce
and chips.

• Per serving 400 kcalories, protein 39g, carbohydrate
15g, fat 21g, saturated fat 8g, fibre 1g, added sugar
14g, salt 1.11g

Made from just five ingredients, but smart enough
for midweek entertaining.

Chicken Rarebits

4 skinless boneless chicken breasts
olive oil, for greasing
140g/5oz cheddar, coarsely grated
1 rounded tbsp wholegrain mustard
3 tbsp milk, preferably full-fat
150g cherry tomatoes, on the vine
broccoli and new potatoes, to serve

Takes 35 minutes • Serves 4

1 Preheat the oven to 200°C/Gas 6/fan oven 180°C. Slice the breasts in half horizontally so you have two thinner pieces that will cook quicker. Lightly oil a shallow baking dish and arrange the chicken in it in a single layer. Mix the cheese, mustard and milk, then pile the mixture on top of each piece of chicken.
2 Throw the tomatoes, still on the vine, all round the chicken, then cook for 20–30 minutes, until the chicken is golden and the tomatoes squashy.
3 Serve with broccoli and new potatoes. Suggest to everyone that they squash the tomatoes on their plates to blend into the cheesy sauce.

• Per serving 316 kcalories, protein 44g, carbohydrate 2g, fat 15g, saturated fat 8g, fibre 1g, added sugar none, salt 1.09g

Chicken thighs are cheap but tasty,
especially in this chunky ratatouille-like sauce.

Spicy Tomato Chicken

2 tbsp seasoned flour
½–1 tsp chilli powder
8 chicken thighs
1 tbsp vegetable oil
1 onion, chopped
600ml/1 pint chicken stock
2 garlic cloves, chopped
2 tbsp tomato purée
2 courgettes, cut into chunks
450g/1lb tomatoes, quartered
mashed potatoes, to serve

Takes 50 minutes • Serves 4

1 Mix together the seasoned flour and chilli powder. Use to coat the chicken thighs. Set aside the remaining seasoned flour. Heat the oil in a large frying pan with a lid. Add the chicken and fry over a moderately high heat for 8–10 minutes, turning once, until browned all over. Transfer to a plate.
2 Add the onion to the pan and cook for 5–6 minutes, stirring occasionally, until softened. Sprinkle in the reserved seasoned flour and cook for 1 minute, stirring continuously. Stir in the stock, garlic and tomato purée.
3 Return the chicken to the pan and bring to the boil. Scatter over the courgettes and tomatoes, stir, cover and simmer for 15–20 minutes. Serve with mashed potatoes.

• Per serving 424 kcalories, protein 33g, carbohydrate 19g, fat 25g, saturated fat 7g, fibre 3g, added sugar none, salt 1.2g

All the flavours of the Sunday roast but easy
enough for a midweek meal.

Baked Chicken with Stuffing Balls

8 chicken thighs
4 carrots, cut into chunks
1 tbsp fresh rosemary or 2 tsp dried
2 tbsp oil
4 potatoes, cut into wedges
1 tbsp plain flour
425ml/¾ pint chicken stock
1 tsp tomato purée

FOR THE STUFFING
1 large onion, chopped
25g/1oz butter
225g/8oz fresh white breadcrumbs
finely grated zest of 1 lemon
2 tsp dried thyme
2 tbsp chopped fresh parsley
1 egg, beaten

Takes 1 hour 40 minutes • Serves 4

1 Preheat the oven to 200°C/Gas 6/fan oven 180°C. Put the chicken and carrots in a roasting tin and sprinkle over the rosemary and half the oil. Put the potatoes in a smaller tin and toss in the remaining oil. Bake the chicken and potatoes for 10 minutes.
2 To make the stuffing, fry the onion in the butter for 5 minutes. Mix in the crumbs, lemon zest, thyme, parsley and egg. Season. Shape into eight balls and put amongst the chicken and carrots after 10 minutes cooking. Bake for 1 hour until cooked and golden.
3 Remove everything from the tins and keep warm. Pour off the fat from the chicken tin, leaving the juices. Stir in the flour and cook for 2 minutes until golden. Add the stock and purée, stirring all the time, until thickened. Serve with the chicken and vegetables.

• Per serving 645 kcalories, protein 50g, carbohydrate 73g, fat 19g, saturated fat 6g, fibre 6g, added sugar none, salt 2.77g

Use ready-made sauce and pastry to save
time on the preparation of this tasty pie.

Easy Chicken and Spinach Pie

2 tbsp olive oil
4 boneless skinless chicken thigh
fillets, cut into 2.5cm/1in chunks
225g/8oz button mushrooms, halved
250g/9oz frozen loose-leaf spinach
225g jar porcini mushroom sauce
375g packet ready-rolled puff pastry
beaten egg, for glazing

Takes 50 minutes • Serves 4

1 Preheat the oven to 220°C/Gas 7/fan oven 200°C. Heat the oil in a frying pan and fry the chicken, stirring occasionally, for 10 minutes until browned. Add the mushrooms and cook for a further 2 minutes. Stir in the spinach and the mushroom sauce and season.
2 Spoon into a 1.7 litre/3 pint pie dish. Brush the rim of the dish with water and lay the sheet of pastry over the filling. Press on to the rim to seal, then trim the pastry edges.
3 Brush with beaten egg and make a small air vent in the middle of the pastry lid with the tip of a knife. Bake for 30–35 minutes until the pastry is crisp, puffed up and golden brown.

• Per serving 603 kcalories, protein 30g, carbohydrate 41g, fat 36g, saturated fat 3g, fibre 2g, added sugar none, salt 1.36g

Get the rice on before you start to stir fry.
This recipe also works well with beef or chicken.

Lamb and Spring Onion Stir Fry

3 tbsp each soy sauce, sherry
and sesame oil
2 tsp wine vinegar
2 garlic cloves
bunch of spring onions
450g/1lb lamb fillet
3 tbsp vegetable oil
cooked rice, to serve

Takes 20 minutes • Serves 4
(easily halved)

1 In a bowl, mix together the soy sauce, sherry, sesame oil and vinegar with four tablespoons of water. Slice the garlic thinly. Cut the spring onions, including the green parts, into 5cm/2in diagonal lengths. Slice the lamb fillet thinly across the grain.

2 Heat the oil in a large frying pan or wok, then add the garlic and stir briefly. Add the lamb and stir fry for 1–2 minutes until browned.

3 Stir in the soy sauce mixture and bubble briefly. Add the spring onions and cook for a few seconds until they just start to soften. Serve with the rice.

• Per serving 435 kcalories, protein 22g, carbohydrate 2g, fat 36g, saturated fat 12g, fibre 1g, added sugar none, salt 2.21g

Use leg of lamb or fillet to be sure the meat is tender.
Marinate the pieces the day before cooking.

Chilli Lamb Skewers

700g/1lb 9oz lean boneless lamb
a small bunch of mint,
stalks removed
1 fresh red chilli, seeded
3 tbsp olive oil
2 small red onions
150g carton low-fat natural yogurt
leafy salad and new potatoes,
to serve

Takes 30 minutes • Serves 4

1 Cut the lamb into bite-sized chunks. Chop the mint and put half in a large bowl and half in a small bowl. Finely chop the chilli and add half to each bowl.

2 Stir three tablespoons of olive oil into the large bowl, season, then add the lamb and turn until glistening and well coated. Finely chop half an onion and add to the small bowl with the yogurt. Season, stir well, then chill until ready to eat (it will keep for a day in the fridge). Cut the rest of the onion into wedges and separate the layers.

3 Thread the lamb on to four large skewers (if wooden, soak them in water first to prevent them burning), with onion in between. Preheat the barbecue or grill and cook the skewers for 6–8 minutes, turning until evenly browned. Serve with the yogurt, a salad and potatoes.

• Per serving 307 kcalories, protein 38g, carbohydrate 6g, fat 15g, saturated fat 7g, fibre none, added sugar none, salt 0.39g

Roughly mashed root vegetables make a colourful accompaniment to roast meat, sausages or chops.

Lamb with Root Veg Crush

2 parsnips, peeled and cubed
1 small swede or 3 carrots, peeled and cubed
600g/1lb 5oz floury potatoes
4 lamb leg steaks (or 8 lamb chops)
olive oil, for brushing
2 tsp dried rosemary
142ml carton soured cream
2 tsp wholegrain mustard

Takes 40 minutes • Serves 4

1 Cook all the vegetables in a large pan of salted boiling water for 15–18 minutes, until tender. Preheat the grill.
2 Brush the lamb with a little oil, sprinkle with rosemary and season. Grill the steaks for 4–5 minutes on each side.
3 Drain the vegetables and crush with a fork, then stir in the soured cream and mustard and season well. Serve with the lamb.

• Per serving 541 kcalories, protein 47g, carbohydrate 41g, fat 22g, saturated fat 11g, fibre 7g, added sugar none, salt 0.46g

A one-pot meal – all you need to serve with
it is a green vegetable, such as buttered cabbage.

Greek Lamb with Potatoes

4 lamb leg steaks or 8 chump
chops, about 750g/
1lb 10oz total weight
2 tsp dried oregano
1kg/2lb 4oz floury potatoes, such as
King Edward, sliced
2 onions, sliced
3 tbsp olive oil
4 fat garlic cloves
300ml/½ pint lamb or chicken
stock or water

Takes 1¼ hours • Serves 4

1 Preheat the oven to 190°C/Gas 5/fan
oven 170°C. Wipe the steaks or chops and
sprinkle with salt, pepper and half the
oregano.

2 Tip the potatoes and onions into a roasting
tin and drizzle over three tablespoons of olive
oil and the rest of the oregano. Season.
Mix until the potatoes and onions are well
coated. Tuck the unpeeled garlic cloves
among the potatoes.

3 Roast the potatoes for 20 minutes until
they are just starting to soften, then put the
chops on top. Pour in the lamb or chicken
stock or water and return to the oven for
30–35 minutes, until the lamb is tender and
the potatoes tinged brown. Make sure everyone gets a garlic clove to squeeze out and
mix with the other ingredients.

• Per serving 545 kcalories, protein 44g, carbohydrate
50g, fat 20g, saturated fat 9g, fibre 4g, added sugar
none, salt 0.61g

Buy a pack of assorted mushrooms in the supermarket,
or mix ordinary and wild mushrooms together.

Lamb's Liver with Mixed Mushrooms

300g/10oz lamb's liver, sliced
2 tbsp seasoned flour
2 tbsp oil
150g pack of wild and exotic
mushrooms, or an equivalent mix
2 garlic cloves, finely chopped
300ml/½ pint chicken stock
good handful chopped fresh parsley
mashed potatoes, to serve

Takes 15 minutes • Serves 2

1 Coat the slices of liver in the seasoned
flour. Heat one tablespoon of the oil in
a frying pan. Add the liver and fry for
30 seconds on each side until just browned.
Remove from the pan and set aside.
2 Pour the remaining tablespoon of oil into
the pan and fry the mushrooms and garlic
for 2–3 minutes. Pour in the stock and return
the liver to the pan. Simmer for 1–2 minutes.
3 Stir in the parsley and season. Serve with
mashed potatoes.

• Per serving 390 kcalories, protein 35g, carbohydrate
17g, fat 21g, saturated fat 4g, fibre 1g, added sugar
none, salt 1.17g

Liven up a simple pork escalope by dipping it in lemon juice then coating with a breadcrumb and herb mixture.

Lemon and Oregano Pork

finely grated zest and juice
of 1 lemon
100g/4oz ready-made natural
coloured breadcrumbs
2 tsp dried oregano
4 pork escalopes
2 tbsp sunflower oil
lemon mayonnaise, potatoes and
green beans, to serve

Takes 20 minutes • Serves 4

1 On a plate, mix together the lemon zest, breadcrumbs and oregano. Pour the lemon juice on to another plate. Dip each pork escalope first in the lemon juice and then into the breadcrumb mixture until well coated.

2 Heat the oil in a large frying pan over a high heat and fry the pork for 3–4 minutes on each side, until the crumbs are crisp and the pork is cooked through.

3 Serve each escalope with a spoonful of lemon mayonnaise, some potatoes and green beans.

• Per serving 291 kcalories, protein 29g, carbohydrate 20g, fat 11g, saturated fat 2g, fibre 1g, added sugar none, salt 0.68g

Make a more sophisticated sauce for the pork by replacing half the stock with red or white wine.

Speedy Pork Pan Fry

500g/1lb 2oz pork tenderloin fillet
1 tbsp plain flour
2 tsp dried rosemary
3 tbsp olive oil
250g/9oz chestnut mushrooms, sliced
1 fat garlic clove, finely chopped
300ml/½ pint vegetable stock
rice or mashed potatoes, and vegetables, to serve

Takes 20 minutes • Serves 4

1 Cut the pork diagonally into finger-thick slices. Tip the flour and rosemary into a plastic bag, season and add the pork. Toss until the meat is well coated.

2 Heat two tablespoons of the oil in a large frying pan. Add the pork and fry for about 3–4 minutes, turning once, until browned on both sides. Remove from the pan.

3 Heat the remaining oil in the pan and fry the mushrooms until they soften, about 2 minutes. Add the garlic and return the pork to the pan with any flour left in the bag. Gradually stir in the stock and bring to the boil. Simmer for 5 minutes or until the pork is cooked. Serve with rice or mashed potatoes, and vegetables.

• Per serving 288 kcalories, protein 30g, carbohydrate 5g, fat 17g, saturated fat 4g, fibre 1g, added sugar none, salt 0.42g

If you can't get these thin meat slices, buy pork steaks. Put between cling film and flatten by bashing with a rolling pin.

Creamy Pork Escalopes

4 tsp plain flour
1 tsp dried sage
4 pork escalopes
2 tbsp oil
knob of butter
1 small onion, finely chopped
225g/8oz chestnut mushrooms, sliced
3 tbsp sherry
200ml carton crème fraîche
noodles, to serve

Takes 30 minutes • Serves 4 (easily halved)

1 Mix the flour with the sage, season, and use to coat the escalopes. Heat one tablespoon of the oil and the butter in a frying pan and fry the pork quickly on each side until nicely browned. Remove from the pan and keep warm.

2 Heat the remaining oil and fry the onion for 1 minute. Add the mushrooms and fry for 2–3 minutes. Add the sherry and let it bubble, scraping up any bits with a wooden spoon.

3 Stir in the crème fraîche. Add the pork and heat through gently for 5 minutes. Serve with noodles.

• Per serving 437 kcalories, protein 28g, carbohydrate 9g, fat 31g, saturated fat 13g, fibre 1g, added sugar none, salt 0.34g

A simple pan fry enriched with caramelised
onions and crème fraîche.

Paprika Pork

2 tbsp olive oil
3 onions, thinly sliced
600g/1lb 5oz pork fillet
2 tbsp paprika
300ml/½ pint chicken or
vegetable stock
100ml crème fraîche
(about half a carton)
freshly chopped parsley, to serve
rice and a green vegetable, to serve

Takes 55 minutes • Serves 4

1 Heat two tablespoons oil in a pan, add
the onions and fry for 10–15 minutes, stirring
occasionally, until softened and lightly
coloured.

2 Cut the pork into bite-sized pieces, then
add to the pan and stir over a fairly high heat
to seal and brown all over. Stir in the paprika,
cook briefly, then add the stock and bring to
the boil.

3 Cover and cook for 30–35 minutes, until
the pork is tender. Stir in the crème fraîche
and simmer for a further 2 minutes. Sprinkle
parsley over the pork, before serving with
rice and a green vegetable.

• Per serving 357 kcalories, protein 36.5g, carbohydrate
11.3g, fat 18.7g, saturated fat 7.6g, fibre 1.3g, added
sugar none, salt 0.52g

Use good-quality ready-made meatballs for these
quick and colourful kebabs.

Meatball Kebabs

350g pack Swedish meatballs
2 courgettes, cut into chunks
2 peppers (1 red and 1 yellow),
seeded and cut into chunks
6 tbsp ready-made honey and
mustard dressing
green salad, to serve

Takes 25 minutes • Serves 4

1 Soak eight wooden kebab sticks in water for 15–20 minutes. Put a griddle pan on the hob over a medium-high heat. While it's heating up, thread the meatballs onto the kebab sticks with the courgette and pepper chunks.
2 Brush them with some of the honey and mustard dressing. Put the skewers on the hot pan and cook for 4–5 minutes on each side – you may need to do this in batches. Brush them occasionally with the dressing.
3 Remove the skewers from the pan and serve with a dressed green salad.

• Per serving 343 kcalories, protein 16g, carbohydrate 12g, fat 26g, saturated fat 8g, fibre 4g, added sugar none, salt 1.46g

Red Thai curry paste is a concentrated mixture
of herbs and spices, flavoured with dried red chillies.

Thai Red Pork Curry

250g/9oz green beans, trimmed
1 tbsp vegetable oil
4 tsp red Thai curry paste
1 tbsp finely chopped fresh
root ginger
500g/1lb 2oz pork fillet, thinly sliced
300ml/½ pint vegetable stock
2 tbsp fish sauce (*nam pla*)
1 tsp light muscovado sugar
400ml can coconut milk
400g can palm hearts, drained,
rinsed and sliced
grated zest and juice of 1 large lime
a handful each of basil and
coriander leaves
rice noodles, to serve

Takes 35 minutes • Serves 4

1 Cook the beans in salted boiling water for 5 minutes, then drain and refresh under cold running water.
2 Heat the oil in a saucepan, add the curry paste and ginger and fry gently until the oil separates out. Tip in the pork and stock, bring to the boil, then simmer for 5 minutes.
3 Add the fish sauce, sugar, coconut milk, palm hearts, lime zest and juice and simmer for a further 5 minutes, adding the beans halfway through. Throw in the basil and coriander and serve with rice noodles.

• Per serving 396 kcalories, protein 32g, carbohydrate 10g, fat 26g, saturated fat 16g, fibre 2g, added sugar 1g, salt 2.29g

Use any boiling sausage, such as German knackwurst or Polish kielbasa. You'll find them with the deli meats.

Smoked Sausage with Leeks

1 tbsp oil
500g/1lb 2oz leeks, trimmed and thickly sliced
1 onion, chopped
6 tbsp dry white wine
6 tbsp chicken stock
2 large, firm, waxy potatoes, peeled and roughly diced
300g/10oz uncooked smoked boiling sausage
3–4 tbsp crème fraîche
chopped fresh parsley, to garnish

Takes 55 minutes • Serves 2

1 Heat the oil in a large pan, add the leeks and onion and cook for 3–4 minutes until just softened. Season, pour in the wine and stock, cover and simmer for 10 minutes.
2 Tip in the diced potatoes, cover the pan again and simmer for 10 minutes or until the potatoes are just tender.
3 Prick the sausage and put it on top of the vegetables. Lower the heat, cover the pan and cook gently for 20 minutes. Lift out the sausage and cut into thick diagonal slices. Stir the crème fraîche into the vegetables and spoon on to plates. Top with the sausage slices and serve garnished with parsley.

• Per serving 727 kcalories, protein 29g, carbohydrate 53g, fat 43g, saturated fat 15g, fibre 9g, added sugar none, salt 2.91g

A tasty combination of potatoes, bacon and melted cheese,
much enjoyed by French skiers.

Tartiflette

750g/1lb 10oz potatoes, peeled
1 onion, finely chopped
25g/1oz butter
drizzle of olive oil
6 rashers smoked back bacon
250g/9oz Reblochon or Pont
l'Evêque cheese
142ml carton single cream
salad, to serve

Takes 45 minutes • Serves 4

1 Preheat the oven to 220°C/Gas 7/fan oven 200°C. Thickly slice the potatoes, then boil in salted water for 8–10 minutes, until just tender. Drain.

2 Fry the onion in the butter and a drizzle of olive oil for 5 minutes. Snip the bacon into pieces with scissors and add to the pan. Cook for a further 5 minutes, until the onion and bacon are lightly coloured.

3 Chop the cheese into chunks, rind and all. Layer half the potatoes in a 1.5 litre/2¾ pint buttered ovenproof dish and scatter over half the onion, bacon and cheese. Lightly season. Repeat the layers, pour the cream evenly over the top and bake for 10–12 minutes until golden. Leave it to rest for 5 minutes and then serve with a salad.

• Per serving 500 kcalories, protein 23g, carbohydrate 30g, fat 32g, saturated fat 19g, fibre 2g, added sugar none, salt 2g

There are lots of interesting textures in this tasty
one-pot meal. Serve it with couscous.

Chickpeas with Bacon and Cabbage

1 tbsp oil
1 onion, roughly chopped
100g/4oz smoked streaky bacon,
roughly chopped
1 small butternut squash, about
400g/14oz, peeled and cubed
300ml/½ pint vegetable or
chicken stock
1 tbsp wholegrain mustard
2 × 400g cans chickpeas, drained
½ green cabbage, shredded
couscous, to serve

Takes 50 minutes • Serves 4

1 Heat the oil in a large saucepan. Add
the onion and cook until golden. Tip in the
bacon and cook, stirring for 5 minutes until
beginning to turn crisp.
2 Stir in the squash and stock. Bring to
the boil, then lower the heat and simmer for
15 minutes, stirring occasionally, until the
squash is almost soft.
3 Stir in the mustard, chickpeas and
cabbage. Cover and cook for a further
5 minutes until the cabbage is just cooked.
Season with plenty of black pepper and
serve with couscous.

• Per serving 297 kcalories, protein 16g, carbohydrate
31g, fat 13g, saturated fat 3g, fibre 9g, added sugar
none, salt 1.89g

You can buy ready-made pancakes from most supermarkets – you'll find them in the bread section.

Ham and Cheese Pancakes

250g/9oz broccoli, cut into small florets
6 ready-made pancakes
6 smoked ham slices
250g whole camembert, chilled
25g/1oz cheddar, grated
4 tomatoes, roughly chopped
salad, to serve

Takes 35 minutes • Serves 4

1 Preheat the oven to 200°C/Gas 6/fan oven 180°C from cold. Cook the broccoli in boiling water for 3 minutes until just tender. Drain and set aside.

2 Put a slice of ham over each pancake. Top with the broccoli. Cut the camembert into thin slices and lay over the broccoli. Season with black pepper. Roll each pancake up like a cigar and put in a single layer in a shallow ovenproof dish.

3 Sprinkle the grated cheddar over the pancakes, then spoon over the chopped tomatoes. Season and bake for 20 minutes until the cheese has melted. Serve with a salad.

• Per serving 379 kcalories, protein 28g, carbohydrate 11g, fat 25g, saturated fat 14g, fibre 3g, added sugar none, salt 2.3g

You could use the same stuffing for other squash too.
Cook in the microwave to save time.

Ham-stuffed Marrow

1 marrow, about 1.5kg/3lb 5oz in weight
25g/1oz butter, cut into cubes
6 tbsp ready-made tomato pasta sauce
about 10 slices wafer-thin ham
4 eggs
85g/3oz Double Gloucester or cheddar, grated

Takes 25 minutes • Serves 4

1 Preheat the oven to 190°C/Gas 5/fan oven 170°C. Peel and halve the marrow and scoop out the seeds. Put in a shallow microwave proof dish, dot with butter and season. Cover with cling film, pierce several times and cook on High for 7 minutes, until tender.

2 Spoon the tomato sauce into each marrow half, then arrange the ham on top. Break two eggs into each half and sprinkle with the cheese.

3 Bake for 12–15 minutes, until the eggs are softly set and the cheese has melted and turned golden.

• Per serving 281 kcalories, protein 20g, carbohydrate 6g, fat 20g, saturated fat 10g, fibre 1g, added sugar none, salt 2g

If you prefer to use cod fillets, add 3–4 minutes to the cooking time, depending on the thickness of the fillets.

Herby Grilled Plaice

2 tbsp olive oil
1 small shallot, finely chopped
finely grated zest of 1 lemon, plus 2 tsp juice
2 tsp chopped fresh dill
2 tsp chopped fresh parsley
2 plaice fillets
steamed new potatoes and peas, to serve

Takes 25 minutes • Serves 2 (easily doubled)

1 Preheat the grill. Put the oil and the shallot in a small pan and cook for 2–3 minutes, until the shallot has softened slightly. Stir in the lemon zest and juice and the chopped herbs, and season.

2 Season the plaice fillets, then lay them skin-side down on a grill pan lined with a little oiled foil. Spoon over the herb oil and grill the fish for 5 minutes (there's no need to turn them).

3 Slide the fish on to warm serving plates and pour over the pan juices. Serve with steamed new potatoes and peas.

• Per serving 230 kcalories, protein 27g, carbohydrate 1g, fat 13g, saturated fat 2g, fibre trace, added sugar none, salt 0.5g

The fish will continue cooking once it's out of the oven,
so if you intend to keep it waiting, slightly undercook it.

Plaice with Bacon Topping

2 tbsp olive oil
4 rashers streaky bacon, chopped
100g/4oz fresh white breadcrumbs
grated zest of 1 lemon
2 tbsp chopped fresh parsley
4 plaice fillets, about 225g/8oz each
new potatoes and green beans,
to serve

Takes 30 minutes • Serves 4

1 Preheat the oven to 230°C/Gas 8/fan oven 210°C. Heat the oil in a frying pan and fry the bacon until crisp. Remove from the heat and stir in the breadcrumbs, lemon zest and parsley. Season with pepper.
2 Line a baking sheet with buttered foil and lay the plaice fillets on top. Sprinkle the crispy bacon topping over the plaice and press down gently.
3 Bake for 7 minutes or until the plaice is cooked and the topping is golden. Serve with new potatoes and green beans.

• Per serving 305 kcalories, protein 30g, carbohydrate 19g, fat 13g, saturated fat 3g, fibre 1g, added sugar none, salt 1.55g

Horseradish really brings out
the flavour of the fish.

Horseradish-crusted Cod with Lentils

200g/7oz puy lentils
1 small bunch parsley
1 tsp sunflower oil
4 heaped tsp horseradish sauce
4 × 175g/6oz cod fillets
4 tbsp fresh white breadcrumbs
4 tbsp half-fat crème fraîche

Takes 40 minutes • Serves 4

1 Place the lentils in a large saucepan with enough cold water to cover them plus an extra couple of inches. Add two whole sprigs of parsley and bring to the boil. Simmer for 25 minutes or until just tender. Discard the parsley.

2 Meanwhile, preheat the oven to 200°C/ Gas 6/fan oven 180°C and grease a non-stick baking tray with the sunflower oil. Spread the horseradish sauce over each fish fillet, then press into the breadcrumbs to coat. Arrange on the baking tray and bake for 15 minutes, until the fish is just cooked through and the breadcrumbs are golden.

3 Meanwhile, roughly chop the remaining parsley. Drain the lentils and toss with the crème fraîche and chopped parsley. Season to taste and serve with the fish.

• Per serving 398 kcalories, protein 47g, carbohydrate 39g, fat 7g, saturated fat 6g, fibre 5g, added sugar 1g, salt 0.86g

Chickpeas, cooked Indian-style with
spinach and chilli, accompany simply grilled fish.

Lemon Cod with Chickpeas

zest and juice of 1 lemon
3 tbsp light olive oil, plus extra
4 × 140g/5oz cod fillets, skinned
1 onion, sliced into thin wedges
250g/9oz packet fresh spinach,
stems trimmed
½–1 tsp dried chilli flakes
420g can chickpeas, rinsed
and drained

Takes 20 minutes • Serves 4

1 Preheat the grill. Mix the lemon zest with one tablespoon of oil. Line a roasting tin with foil, oil lightly and arrange the fillets on it. Brush with the lemon oil. Season and grill for 8–10 minutes until cooked (no need to turn).
2 Meanwhile, heat the rest of the oil and fry the onion until golden. Add the spinach and cook until wilted. Stir in the chilli flakes. Tip in the chickpeas and one tablespoon of lemon juice and heat through. Season.
3 Spoon the chickpea mixture on to hot plates and serve the fish on top. Drizzle with a little extra oil or lemon juice.

• Per serving 306 kcalories, protein 32g, carbohydrate 14g, fat 13g, saturated fat 2g, fibre 4g, added sugar none, salt 1.03g

A simple, savoury finish for plain salmon fillets,
cooked in just one pan.

Honey and Soy Salmon

1 tbsp wholegrain mustard
2 tsp clear honey
1 tbsp soy sauce
1 tsp olive oil
4 boneless skinless salmon fillets,
about 140g/5oz each in weight
100ml/3½fl oz vegetable stock
1 bunch of spring onions, halved
lengthways, then cut into strips
boiled rice, to serve

Takes 20 minutes • Serves 4

1 Mix together the mustard, honey and
soy sauce in a small bowl. Heat the oil in
a frying pan. Add the salmon fillets and fry
for 5 minutes, turning halfway through, until
almost cooked.
2 Pour the soy mixture over the salmon and
bring just to the boil. Add the stock and mix
lightly with the pan juices.
3 Sprinkle over the spring onion strips and
let the liquid bubble for 1–2 minutes, until
the onions are heated through. Serve with
boiled rice.

• Per serving 281 kcalories, protein 29g, carbohydrate
4g, fat 17g, saturated fat 3g, fibre 1g, added sugar
2g, salt 1.08g

A luxurious dish, deceptively easy
to prepare and perfect for entertaining.

Salmon with Almonds and Cheese

4 × 175g/6oz salmon fillets
50g/2oz softened butter
4 tbsp slivered or flaked almonds
4 tbsp chopped fresh parsley
50g/2oz gruyère or emmental,
coarsely grated
potatoes and a green salad or
broccoli, to serve

Takes 30 minutes • Serves 4

1 Preheat the oven to 190°C/Gas 5/fan oven 170°C. Season the salmon steaks all over. Liberally butter a shallow ovenproof dish big enough to take the fish in one layer. Smear the fillets with the remaining butter.
2 Mix the almonds, parsley and the gruyère or emmental, then press on to the top of the steaks.
3 Bake for 15–20 minutes, until the topping is crisp and golden and the salmon cooked. Serve with potatoes and a green salad or broccoli.

• Per serving 523 kcalories, protein 41g, carbohydrate 1g, fat 39g, saturated fat 15g, fibre 1g, added sugar none, salt 0.66g

Whipping cream is rich enough to heat without separating,
but has less fat than double cream (35% instead of 42%).

Salmon with Tarragon Cream

2 salmon fillets
1 tbsp vegetable oil
1 finely chopped shallot or
½ small onion
2 tbsp chopped fresh tarragon
6 tbsp whipping cream
2 tbsp chopped fresh parsley
lemon wedges, to garnish
new potatoes and green beans,
to serve

Takes 25 minutes • Serves 2
(easily doubled)

1 Preheat the oven to 180°C/Gas 4/fan oven 160°C. Season the salmon steaks on both sides. Heat one tablespoon of oil in a frying pan (preferably non-stick) until fairly hot. Add the salmon, flesh-side down, and fry quickly for about 3 minutes until lightly browned. Turn over and fry the skin side for 2 minutes.

2 Transfer to a shallow ovenproof dish and sprinkle over the shallot or onion and the tarragon. Spoon over the cream and season.

3 Cook in the oven for 12–15 minutes until the salmon is cooked. Sprinkle with chopped parsley, transfer to warm plates and garnish with lemon wedges. Serve with new potatoes and green beans.

• Per serving 448 kcalories, protein 32g, carbohydrate 3g, fat 34g, saturated fat 14g, fibre 1g, added sugar none, salt 0.23g

As a variation, instead of the garlic and herb soft cheese, try using the black pepper variety.

Salmon Watercress Puffs

75g bag watercress
375g packet ready-rolled puff pastry, thawed
4 skinless salmon fillets, 140g/5oz each in weight
grated zest of 1 lemon
150g packet soft cheese with garlic and herbs
milk or beaten egg, for brushing
new potatoes, to serve

Takes 30 minutes • Serves 4

1 Preheat the oven to 200°C/Gas 6/fan oven 180°C. Put half the watercress in a pan with a tablespoon of water and cook for a few minutes until wilted. Drain and chop.
2 Roll out the pastry to a 38 × 30cm/ 15 × 12in rectangle. Cut in quarters to make four smaller rectangles. Put a salmon fillet on one half of each rectangle. Scatter over a little lemon zest and season. Divide the cheese and cooked watercress between the fillets. Damp the pastry edges with a little milk or egg, fold over the pastry and seal to enclose the filling.
3 Put the pastry parcels on a baking sheet and brush with milk or egg. Bake for 20 minutes until the pastry is puffed and golden. Serve with the remaining watercress and new potatoes.

• Per serving 675 kcalories, protein 38g, carbohydrate 36g, fat 43g, saturated fat 3g, fibre trace, added sugar none, salt 1.21g

Choose a salad that contains radicchio and a mixture
of white and red cabbage to give this dish a lovely crunch.

Salmon and Salad Stir Fry

1 tbsp oil
5cm/2in piece fresh root
ginger, grated
450g/1lb salmon fillet, skinned and
cut into 2.5cm/1in cubes
1 bunch of spring onions, cut into
4cm/1½in lengths
150ml/¼ pint vegetable stock
200g bag mixed salad leaves
2 tbsp light soy sauce
steamed or boiled rice, to serve

Takes 25 minutes • Serves 4

1 Heat the oil in a frying pan, add the ginger
and cook for 30 seconds, stirring. Season
the salmon, add to the pan and cook for
5 minutes, turning once until just cooked
through and beginning to brown.
2 Remove the salmon from the pan and
keep warm. Add the spring onions and stir
fry for 3–4 minutes until just soft.
3 Pour over the stock and bring to the boil.
Tip in the salad and cook for 1 minute to
wilt. Return the salmon to the pan, tip in
the soy sauce and serve hot from the pan
with rice.

• Per serving 248 kcalories, protein 24g, carbohydrate
3g, fat 16g, saturated fat 3g, fibre 1g, added sugar
none, salt 0.26g

Don't miss out on trout because you don't like bones.
Fillets are easy to eat with salad.

Trout with Warm Potato Salad

600g/1lb 5oz new potatoes
225g/8oz broccoli,
cut into small florets
4 trout fillets (about 100g/4oz
each in weight)
3 tbsp olive oil, plus extra
for brushing
1 tbsp white wine vinegar
12 cherry tomatoes, halved
2 tbsp toasted flaked almonds

Takes 20 minutes • Serves 4

1 Wash the potatoes and cut each in half or quarters if large. Cook in salted boiling water for 12 minutes, adding the broccoli for the last 3 minutes of cooking time.
2 Preheat the grill to high. Put the trout fillets on the grill pan. Brush each with a little oil and season. Grill for 3–4 minutes.
3 Drain the potatoes and broccoli well. Tip into a bowl. Whisk together the three tablespoons of oil and the vinegar. Add to the hot vegetables along with the tomatoes, almonds and a little seasoning. Toss well and serve with the grilled trout.

• Per serving 378 kcalories, protein 26g, carbohydrate 26g, fat 19g, saturated fat 2g, fibre 4g, added sugar none, salt 0.43g

The perfect late-night snack for one.

Or multiply the recipe for a weekend family brunch.

Smoked Salmon Muffins

1 English muffin
knob of unsalted butter, plus
extra for buttering
2 eggs
1 tbsp milk
25g/1oz smoked salmon trimmings
1 tsp freshly snipped chives

Takes 10 minutes • Serves 1

1 Preheat the grill to hot. Split and toast the muffin until golden. Spread with butter and keep warm. Meanwhile, lightly beat the eggs and milk together in a bowl and season with freshly ground black pepper.

2 Melt the butter in a pan and when foaming pour in the eggs. Cook over a low heat, pulling the cooked egg from the edges of the pan into the centre until the egg begins to set.

3 Stir in the smoked salmon and chives and cook for a further 1–2 minutes. Pile on top of the toasted buttered muffin halves and serve.

• Per serving 502 kcalories, protein 26g, carbohydrate 34g, fat 30g, saturated fat 13g, fibre 1g, added sugar none, salt 2.39g

This easy family meal cooks brilliantly –
and quickly – in the microwave.

Smoked Haddock with Chive Potatoes

950g/2lb 2oz potatoes (such as
King Edward)
1 small onion, thinly sliced
25g/1oz butter
300ml/½ pint vegetable stock
140g/5oz frozen peas
142ml carton single cream
4 boneless skinless smoked haddock
fillets, each about 140g/5oz
2 tbsp freshly snipped chives

Takes 30 minutes • Serves 4

1 Peel and thickly slice the potatoes. Put into a large microwave proof shallow dish, about 2.8 litre/5 pint capacity, with the onion, and season. Dot with half the butter and pour over the stock.

2 Cover loosely with cling film and microwave on High for 15 minutes, stirring halfway through, until the potatoes are just tender. Gently stir in the peas and pour over the cream.

3 Put the smoked haddock on top of the potatoes and dot each piece with the remaining butter. Sprinkle with the chives. Cover with cling film and cook for 5 minutes on High, until the fish is just cooked through. Serve immediately.

• Per serving 413 kcalories, protein 34g, carbohydrate 41g, fat 14g, saturated fat 8g, fibre 5g, added sugar none, salt 3.15g

Use raw king prawns to make this simple
but extra-special supper.

Gently Spiced Prawn Curry

10 raw king prawns, in their shells
4 tsp vegetable oil
1 tsp mustard seeds
1 small onion, finely chopped
1 tbsp finely chopped fresh
root ginger
1 plump garlic clove, finely chopped
¼ tsp ground turmeric
¼ tsp hot chilli powder
½ tsp ground coriander
2 fresh bay leaves
1 small green chilli, seeded and
thinly sliced
200ml carton coconut cream
1 lime, halved
basmati rice and lime wedges,
to serve

Takes 30 minutes • Serves 2

1 Peel the prawns and set aside. Heat the oil in a medium frying pan. Fry the mustard seeds until they crackle and pop. Add the onion. Fry, stirring, until golden. Add the ginger and garlic. Stir fry for 1 minute.
2 Add the turmeric, chilli powder and coriander and stir fry for 30 seconds. Add the bay leaves and chilli. Stir over a medium heat for 1 minute. Pour in 150ml/¼ pint water and bubble for a minute.
3 Add the prawns and spoon over the sauce. Lower the heat and simmer for 3–4 minutes, until the prawns are cooked. Pour in the coconut cream, warm through and squeeze in the juice of half a lime. Season with salt. Serve with basmati rice and lime wedges.

• Per serving 519 kcalories, protein 23g, carbohydrate 12g, fat 42g, saturated fat 31g, fibre 1g, added sugar none, salt 3.08g

Prawns and eggs are a surprisingly successful combination.
Try this for a late supper for two.

Prawn and Spring Onion Omelette

1 tbsp olive oil
4 eggs
100g/4oz peeled cooked prawns
4 spring onions, trimmed and
thinly sliced
tomato salad and crusty bread,
to serve

Takes 10 minutes • Serves 2
(easily doubled)

1 Preheat the grill. Heat the oil in a frying pan. Lightly beat the eggs and season. Pour into the frying pan and cook over a medium heat for 30 seconds until the egg mixture starts to set.

2 Using a fork, gently draw some of the egg mixture from the edge into the middle. Sprinkle over the prawns and spring onions and cook for 2 minutes.

3 Transfer the pan to the grill and cook for a further 1–2 minutes until golden brown. Fold the omelette over. Cut in half and serve with a tomato salad and crusty bread.

• Per serving 250 kcalories, protein 24g, carbohydrate none, fat 17g, saturated fat 4g, fibre none, added sugar none, salt 1.36g

This is a breeze to make – ready-made pancakes and a
sauce made from a carton of soup make it simplicity itself.

Seafood Pancakes

25g/1oz butter
1 onion, chopped
2 celery sticks, chopped
1 tbsp plain flour
500g carton fresh watercress soup
142ml carton double cream
700g/1lb 9oz mixture of fresh fish,
such as cod fillet and salmon,
cut into chunks, and seafood
such as prawns or mussels
2 packs (12) ready-made pancakes
50g/2oz mature cheddar, grated

Takes 40 minutes • Serves 6

1 Preheat the oven to 200°C/Gas 6/fan
oven 180°C from cold. Heat the butter in
a pan and fry the onion and celery for
5 minutes until softened. Stir in the flour
and cook for 1 minute more. Add half the
soup and half the cream. Bring to the boil.
2 Add the fish and simmer for 5 minutes,
stirring gently, until the fish is just cooked.
Season with black pepper. Spoon the
mixture into the centre of the pancakes
and fold into square parcels. Arrange in a
shallow ovenproof dish.
3 Heat the remaining soup and cream,
spoon over the pancakes and sprinkle with
the cheese. Bake for 20–25 minutes until
the cheese is golden.

• Per serving 571 kcalories, protein 28g, carbohydrate
28g, fat 39g, saturated fat 20g, fibre 2g, added sugar
none, salt 1.99g

If using an electric hand whisk, don't over-whip the cream or it will be too stiff to mix easily with the meringue and fruit.

Raspberry Syllabub Eton Mess

3 ready-made meringue nests
350g/12oz fresh raspberries
4 tbsp dry white wine
85g/3oz caster sugar
finely grated zest and juice
of 1 lemon
284ml carton double cream
icing sugar, for dusting

Takes 10 minutes • Serves 4

1 Break the meringues into pieces in a bowl. Add 250g/9oz raspberries.
2 In a large bowl, stir together the wine, sugar, lemon zest and juice, until the sugar has dissolved. Using a wire whisk, gradually whisk in the cream, until it just holds its shape.
3 Spoon the syllabub over the meringue and raspberries and gently stir together. Do not overmix or the cream will turn pink. Spoon into a serving bowl, scatter with the remaining raspberries and chill. Dust with icing sugar just before serving.

• Per serving 502 kcalories, protein 3g, carbohydrate 46g, fat 34g, saturated fat 21g, fibre 2g, added sugar 39g, salt 0.12g

Use a potato peeler to make shavings from a chocolate bar.
Or use chocolate flake instead.

Chocolate Cream Pots

140g/5oz dark chocolate
142ml carton whipping cream
5 tbsp Irish cream liqueur
250g carton mascarpone
chocolate shavings,
to decorate (optional)

Takes 20 minutes • Serves 4

1 Break the chocolate into a bowl and microwave on High for about 2 minutes or until melted. Alternatively, melt in a bowl set over simmering water, making sure the bottom of the bowl doesn't touch the water. Stir and set aside to cool.
2 Whisk the cream to soft peaks and whisk in the Irish cream liqueur. Beat the mascarpone until smooth, then beat in the Irish cream liqueur mixture. Pour in the cooled chocolate and stir lightly together to make a swirly pattern.
3 Spoon the mixture into 150ml/¼ pint pots or ramekins. Cover generously with chocolate shavings, if liked, and serve.

• Per serving 703 kcalories, protein 5g, carbohydrate 37g, fat 59g, saturated fat 34g, fibre 1g, added sugar 32g, salt 0.24g

A really quick dessert combining no-cook ingredients.
Try it with other fruits too.

Apricot Cookies 'n' Cream

411g can apricots in natural juice
284ml carton extra-thick
double cream
200g carton Greek yogurt
10 chocolate biscuits, such as
chocolate covered oat biscuits or
chocolate digestives
1 tsp ground cinnamon
2 tbsp demerara sugar

Takes 10 minutes • Serves 4

1 Drain the apricots, reserving half of the juice. Roughly chop the apricots and divide between four glasses. Spoon over the reserved juice.

2 In a bowl, mix together the cream and the yogurt. Roughly chop the biscuits and stir into the cream mixture, then spoon over the apricots.

3 Mix together the cinnamon and the sugar. Sprinkle over the cream mixture and serve straightaway.

• Per serving 649 kcalories, protein 8g, carbohydrate 47g, fat 49g, saturated fat 29g, fibre 2g, added sugar 19g, salt 0.66g

An easily assembled dessert. Make it boozy by adding
a little kirsch or brandy to the cherry syrup.

Black Forest Trifle

200g ready-made Madeira cake
425g can pitted black cherries
in syrup
1 chocolate flake
100g packet plain chocolate drops
400g carton fresh custard
200ml carton crème fraîche

Takes 20 minutes, plus chilling •
Serves 4 generously

1 Cut the cake into thick slices and use
to line the base of a 2.5 litre/4½ pint serving
bowl. Cut three cherries in half and reserve,
and spoon the rest over the cake along with
the syrup. Crumble half the flake over the
cherries and scatter over half the chocolate
drops.
2 Heat the remaining chocolate drops in
a microwave proof bowl on Medium for
2 minutes, stirring halfway through, until
melted. Cool for 5 minutes, then whisk into
the custard gradually, until you have a smooth
chocolate custard. Pour over the cherries.
3 Spoon the crème fraîche over the custard.
Sprinkle with the reserved cherries and
crumble over the remaining flake. Chill until
ready to serve.

• Per serving 478 kcalories, protein 7g, carbohydrate
59g, fat 25g, saturated fat 14g, fibre 1g, added sugar
16g, salt 0.57g

An instant iced dessert, guaranteed to
make a refreshing finale to a meal.

Summer Fruits Ice Yogurt

500g bag of frozen mixed
summer fruits
2 × 200g carton Greek yogurt
100ml/3½fl oz (about 7 tbsp) fresh
orange juice
1 tbsp icing sugar
biscuits, shortbread or almond thins,
to serve (optional)

Takes 10 minutes • Serves 4

1 Put the frozen fruits, yogurt, orange juice
and icing sugar in a food processor. Whizz
until blended, but make sure the fruit still has
some texture.
2 Scrape the mixture from the sides of the
processor and whizz again. Repeat until the
mixture looks like frozen yogurt.
3 Spoon into chunky glasses and serve
immediately, with biscuits, if liked.

• Per serving 184 kcalories, protein 8g, carbohydrate
18g, fat 9g, saturated fat 6g, fibre 3g, added sugar
7g, salt 0.2g

Keep the heat quite high during the cooking so
the sugar melts to produce a sticky sauce.

Fried Rum Bananas

knob of butter
4 bananas, sliced diagonally into
four pieces
4 tbsp rum or brandy
4 tbsp double cream or
crème fraîche
2 tbsp light muscovado sugar

Takes 10 minutes • Serves 4

1 Melt the butter in a large frying pan.
When the butter is foaming, fry the bananas
for 2 minutes, then turn them and pour in
the rum or brandy. Fry for 1–2 minutes more
until browned.
2 Stir the cream or crème fraîche and sugar
into the pan and warm through for 1 minute.
3 Divide the bananas between four
plates and spoon over the sauce. Serve
immediately.

• Per serving 237 kcalories, protein 2g, carbohydrate
32g, fat 9g, saturated fat 5g, fibre 1g, added sugar
8g, salt 0.11g

A sweet and gooey open sandwich made from
storecupboard ingredients in 10 minutes.

Choc-o-nut Pear Toasts

25g/1oz butter
2 pears, peeled, cored and sliced
25g/1oz light muscovado sugar
juice of 1 orange
4 thick slices white bread
4 tbsp chocolate nut spread

Takes 10 minutes • Serves 4

1 Preheat the grill. Melt the butter in a frying
pan, then add the pear slices and fry quickly
for about 5 minutes, until lightly browned and
softened.
2 Stir in the sugar, then add the orange juice
and bubble until it forms a syrupy sauce.
3 Toast the bread on both sides. Spoon the
chocolate nut spread over one side of each
slice. Put on serving plates and spoon on
the hot pears. Serve straightaway.

• Per serving 262 kcalories, protein 4g, carbohydrate
36g, fat 12g, saturated fat 4g, fibre 2g, added sugar
7g, salt 0.52g

Try nectarines or peaches served warm for a change.
You'll love this combination of fruit and soft cheese.

Roasted Stuffed Nectarines

4 nectarines
8 gingernut biscuits
25g/1oz butter
2 tsp clear honey
finely grated zest and juice
of 1 orange
225g/8oz soft cheese
2 tbsp caster sugar

Takes 25 minutes • Serves 4

1 Preheat the oven to 180°C/Gas 4/fan oven 160°C. Halve the nectarines and remove and discard the stones. Put the nectarines flesh-side up in a shallow, ovenproof dish.
2 Put the biscuits in a plastic bag and roughly crush with a rolling pin. Melt the butter in a small pan over a low heat. Stir the crushed biscuits into the melted butter along with the honey. Spoon a little of the mixture on top of each nectarine.
3 Pour the orange juice over the nectarines and bake for 20 minutes. Meanwhile, put the soft cheese in a bowl and beat in the sugar and orange zest. Serve with the warm nectarines and juices.

• Per serving 416 kcalories, protein 8g, carbohydrate 43g, fat 25g, saturated fat 4g, fibre 3g, added sugar 14g, salt 1g

Based on the Baked Alaska idea – baked ice cream
and meringue – but using a moist ginger cake.

Baked Jamaica

227g can pineapple chunks in
natural juice
1 ready-made Jamaica ginger cake,
sliced horizontally
3 egg whites
175g/6oz light muscovado sugar
500ml carton vanilla ice cream

Takes 20 minutes • Serves 4

1 Preheat the oven to 220°C/Gas 7/fan
oven 200°C. Drain the pineapple, reserving
three tablespoons of juice. Put the ginger
cake slices side by side in a rectangular
shallow ovenproof dish. Drizzle over the
pineapple juice and pineapple chunks.
2 Whisk the egg whites until stiff. Whisk in
the sugar, a tablespoon at a time, whisking
well between each addition until the
meringue is thick and glossy.
3 Slice the ice cream and cover the fruit
and sponge with it, pressing down to level.
Completely cover with the meringue, swirling
the top with a fork. Bake for 5 minutes until
golden. Serve at once.

• Per serving 484 kcalories, protein 9g, carbohydrate
85g, fat 14g, saturated fat 7g, fibre 1g, added sugar
59g, salt 0.53g

Try this easy-mix crumble topping with other fruits too.
A microwave speeds cooking but is not essential.

Oaty Red Fruit Crumble

4 eating apples, peeled,
cored and chopped
300g can summer fruits in syrup
100g/4oz butter
50g/2oz light muscovado sugar
140g/5oz porridge oats
ready-made custard, ice cream or
cream, to serve

Takes 40 minutes • Serves 4

1 Preheat the oven to 190°C/Gas 5/fan oven 170°C from cold. Mix together the apples, summer fruits and their syrup in a 850ml/1½ pint microwave proof pie dish. Microwave on High for 5–8 minutes (depending on the wattage), stirring halfway through, until the apples are cooked. Alternatively, cook in a pan on the hob, stirring for 12–15 minutes.

2 Melt the butter in a bowl on Medium in the microwave for 1–2 minutes (or in a small pan), until just melted. Stir in the sugar and oats. Spoon over the fruit.

3 Bake for 20 minutes until the topping is golden and the filling is just bubbling. Serve with custard, ice cream or cream.

• Per serving 478 kcalories, protein 5g, carbohydrate 65g, fat 24g, saturated fat 14g, fibre 5g, added sugar 19g, salt 0.56g

Index

Picture credits and recipe credits

BBC Worldwide would like to thank the following for providing photographs. While every effort has been made to trace and acknowledge all photographers, we would like to apologise should there be any errors or omissions.

Marie-Louise Avery p69, p113, p191; Iain Bagwell p31, p143; Jean Cazals p17, p55, p79; Ken Field p19, p37, p41, p97, p111, p149; David Jordan p27; David Munns p33, p39, p99, p165; William Reavell p23; Craig Robertson p45, p103, p193; Simon Smith p35, p43, p91, p179; Roger Stowell p13, p15, p25, p29, p47, p49, p51, p53, p57, p61, p67, p73, p75, p83, p85, p95, p101, p105, p107, p109, p115, p117, p119, p121, p123, p129, p131, p135, p139, p141, p145, p151, p153, p159, p161, p163, p167, p169, p175, p177, p181, p185, p189, p197, p199, p201, p203, p205, p207, p209, p211; Sam Stowell p93, p171; Martin Thompson p125, p157; Martin Thompson and Philip Webb p127; Ian Wallace p195; Philip Webb p21, p63, p187; Simon Wheeler p65, p71, p77, p81, p87, p133, p137, p147, p155, p173; Jonathan Whittaker p11, p59, p89; Geoff Wilkinson p183

All the recipes in this book have been created by the editorial teams on *BBC Good Food Magazine* and *BBC Vegetarian Good Food Magazine*.

Angela Boggiano, Lorna Brash, Sara Buenfeld, Mary Cadogan, Gilly Cubitt, Barney Desmazery, Joanna Farrow, Rebecca Ford, Silvana Franco, Catherine Hill, Jane Lawrie, Clare Lewis, Sara Lewis, Liz Martin, Kate Moseley, Orlando Murrin, Vicky Musselman, Angela Nilsen, Justine Pattison, Jenny White and Jeni Wright.